W9-BPQ-579

SAFE
IN THE
STORM

*The Grace of God,
In the Midst of Cancer*

STEPHEN B. HATCHER

Scripture quotations denoted "ESV" are taken from the Holy Bible, English Standard Version, copyright © 2001 by Crossway Bibles, a publishing ministry of Good News Publishers. Used by permission. All rights reserved.

Scripture quotations denoted "NIV" are taken from the Holy Bible, New International Version. Copyright © 1973, 1978, 1984 by International Bible Society. Used by permission of Zondervan. All rights reserved.

Scripture quotations denoted "NASV" are taken from the New American Standard Bible. Copyright © 1960, 1963, 1968, 1971, 1972, 1973, 1975, 1995 by The Lockman Foundation. Used by permission. All rights reserved.

Editor: Mike Purswell, Nashville, Tennessee

Copyright © 2012 Stephen B. Hatcher
All rights reserved.
ISBN-10: 0988442108
EAN-13: 9780988442108

Thank you to all who have prayed for me throughout
my journey and who continue to do so.

Special thanks to Mike and Carl whose
assistance has been invaluable.

And very special thanks to Becky, whose intuition,
insight and direction
at so many points while I was writing, both
set me on the right path and then kept me there.
Thanks for being my partner on this journey. There is no one
I would rather have beside me.

To God be the glory.

Table of Contents

Prologue

The nurse on the other end of the line said the doctor wanted to see me the next day. I told her that I already had an appointment to go over the test results next week, after I got back from my trip. She said simply, "The doctor wants to see you tomorrow." Ever had that call? Those words are code for "something is bad in the report and we need to deal with it"; words you don't want to hear.

The MRI films showed a large tumor on my spine. "I'm not an oncologist, but I would suspect it is cancerous." Cancer? Was I in some sort of dream? "Mr. Hatcher, do you understand what I am saying?" Yes, all too well. It was like a big eraser wiped everything off the board of my future. The board was empty; now what?

I had made it to my mid-fifties without any really significant health issues. I was one of those guys who ate right, exercised regularly and maintained a healthy balance in life. Sure, I have some knee and ankle problems from sports injuries or taking the Boy Scouts hiking on the Appalachian Trail, but nothing too dramatic. You don't get too many injuries practicing law or leading Bible studies.

Cancer. Was this part of God's plan too? If so, why? Did I do something wrong? During the first twenty-four hours the initial questions screamed inside my head: what about Becky, the kids, friends, family...? How much time do I have and why did I waste so much of it assuming I would never face something like this? Then bigger questions: is God who I thought He was? Can I trust Him; can I believe? Finally the pleas... God, please let me stay in the game; there is so much I still want to do... need to do.

Take a journey with me. I want to show you how an unexpected challenge showed me that the God I already knew was exactly who I thought He was... only better; so much better.

What you are about to read is the account of my walk through cancer and what God taught me as I went through spine surgery, chemotherapy, radiation and, eventually, a stem cell transplant. My story is written between the lines of emails that I sent to faithful friends who were praying for me.

CHAPTER ONE

How the Journey Began

July 20

If you are reading this while sitting at your desk, please do not visibly react since I am only sending it to a select few of you at the office. I met with the orthopedic surgeon this afternoon to review my MRI results. This may be news to a couple of you, but I have been having back pain and have lost some feeling in my legs. I attributed it to pulling out a stump in the back yard in April. I had an extensive MRI on Monday. It turns out that I have some form of tumor on my spine at the T-7 vertebra. I am out the next two days visiting my mom in Tennessee, but I will be having a full CAT scan, body scan and bone scan Monday or Tuesday. I would like to keep everything confidential until I see those results next Wednesday. I will give you an update then. I will certainly be having back surgery to remove the growth, whatever it is, within the next week. I will obviously be updating everyone then and will likely spread the news to the firm as a whole.

Until then, I rejoice to know that all of you love me and will be praying for me. There is no need to email me to tell me that; I already know it. I will be in Monday morning, but will not know anything new at that point. Thanks for your prayers and please keep this confidential for now.

Steve

In April of 2011, I began having back pain. I had been doing some heavy yard work and thought the pain was just a pulled muscle. As most guys do, I nursed it for a while, trying to allow it to heal over time. By June, it had not improved and my general practitioner referred me to a sports therapist who, when therapy didn't help either, referred me to an orthopedic surgeon. In July an MRI showed some form of tumor on my spine just below my shoulder blades, as well as three other smaller spots on my spine. By this time, I had begun to feel weakness in my legs, I was having some difficulty walking and I was carrying a long umbrella just in case I needed it for stability. The orthopedic surgeon suspected that the larger tumor was constricting the spinal cord and that it was cancerous. He immediately ordered a full CT and bone scan, scheduled for five days later.

My wife's brother is a surgeon who trained at the Mayo Clinic in Rochester, MN. He connected us with the specialists at the Mayo Clinic in Jacksonville, Florida, two hours from where we live near Orlando. I was walking out of the imaging clinic after finishing the CT and bone scan when I received a call from a Mayo oncologist, who said he had an opening to see me on the very next day. This was a timing miracle with God's fingerprints all over it.

The next morning, my wife Becky and I picked up the films and discs from my scans and drove to Jacksonville. The Mayo oncologist looked at the scan data and also the MRI pictures. He confirmed that the tumor was causing a serious constriction of the spinal column. He said that I had two dangers: multiple myeloma (cancer) and paraplegia (loss of the use of my legs). The paraplegia actually concerned him more than the cancer. He called a neurosurgeon, who had me come immediately to his office on the Mayo campus. The neurosurgeon also looked at the MRI, put me through several leg strength tests (which I thought I had passed with flying colors) and then showed me what looked like a 40 to 50 percent constriction on the spinal cord! He strongly encouraged me not to wait, but to have the surgery the *very next day* to remove the tumor. This specialist went on to explain that he was the Chief of Neurosurgery, and that he would do the operation himself! I could not have been in better hands. God's fingerprints were evident again.

To add a little extra drama to the situation, the night before my surgery, our first grandchild was delivered by emergency C-section! After the delivery, the doctor explained that our daughter-in-law had an unusual condition called *vasa previa*, which causes the vessels that supply blood to the baby to break at the same time that the mother's water breaks. If they had not been at the hospital when the water broke, she would have lost the baby. God, in His grace, saved that little child. The next morning, he would guide the hands of the surgeon to save my spinal cord.

My surgery was successful, but my surgeon explained that the operation was MUCH more extensive than he had thought it would be. The myeloma had destroyed the rear of my T-7 vertebra, so he had to remove that portion. Fortunately, the stability of the spine is in the front, not the rear. Again, God's grace was clearly present.

It had been a whirlwind; exactly seven days from the MRI results to testing, referrals and successful surgery. Becky and I were trying to catch our breath. A new storm had begun in our lives. We could only wait to see how big it would be and, more importantly, how God would get us through it.

CHAPTER TWO

I Am Small

August 22

First, let me thank you for your prayers! God continues to be very gracious to me as I walk along this path. We stayed in Jacksonville for a week, just to be close to Mayo after the surgery. When we returned to Orlando, we immediately made a quick trip to see our new granddaughter; what a blessing she is! My recovery from the surgery continues and I am weaning myself off the pain medications. I have now had two rounds of chemotherapy and the negative impacts have been very minimal. Two nights after the first round, I had a fever spike (followed by a stress-filled trip to the emergency room) and a lot of fatigue the next day, but nothing major. It is now the third day after the second round and I have had no negative results other than fatigue.

God has taught me a great deal during these initial weeks. First, He is much bigger than I thought He was. I am also much smaller than I thought I was. I think He increases our knowledge of both our limitations and His immeasurable abilities every time our lives take a major detour. It is one thing to acknowledge it in your mind, but quite another to experience it.

My empathy for those I see with health issues or physical limitations has also virtually exploded. Yes, there is a difference between empathy (knowing what someone else is experiencing) and sympathy (feeling for someone else who is going through something that you are not).

I met with the radiologist who will do my radiation treatments this morning. It sounds like I will have only ten low-dose treatments over a two-week period. I could have some burning of the esophagus, due to its proximity to the T-7 site, but that will not show up until week three and he hopes (so do I!) that it will be minimal. That impact could last for another three weeks after the radiation stops, so if I am a little grouchy, you'll know why!

The journey will continue. I am so very thankful that you are in this with me. Your encouragement is incredible.

Steve

There I was, full of energy and the picture of health. I was running, working out and playing sports. I was even pulling stumps from the back yard with my bare hands! I was successful, happily married; I had wonderful children and enjoyed respect both in the church and in my profession.

Then cancer showed up. Cancer doesn't care who you are or what you have accomplished. In a real sense, neither should we. We are small and fragile, whether we acknowledge it or not. Our next breath and our next heartbeat are both completely dependent upon the grace of a loving and all-powerful God. We cannot even worry ourselves to a longer life: "And which of you by being anxious can add a single hour to his span of life?" (Matthew 6:27; Luke 12:25 ESV)

We need to admit who we are and who God is. Deep inside we know the truth. The reality of our own weakness surfaces especially during trials, when we run and cling to His feet. But we need to acknowledge it always;

it is simply good spiritual health. As Jesus told us: "you will know the truth, and the truth will set you free." (John 8:32 ESV)

The Old Testament writers had a better concept of the majesty and awesome power of God. In an agrarian society, scraping together a life under harsh conditions, without all of the ease and comfort that we have in our day and age, it was easier to see how small you were compared to the God of the heavens:

Be not rash with your mouth, nor let your heart be hasty to utter a word before God, for God is in heaven and you are on earth. Therefore let your words be few. (Ecclesiastes 5:2 ESV)

"Behold, I am of small account; what shall I answer you? I lay my hand on my mouth." (Job 40:4 ESV)

Those who refuse to accept God try to convince us that we are the masters of the universe! They tell us we are rulers of our own destiny, not subject to any force save ourselves and limited only by the strength of our own will. We need to admit the truth:

You say, 'I am rich; I have acquired wealth and do not need a thing.' But you do not realize that you are wretched, pitiful, poor, blind, and naked. (Revelation 3:17 NIV)

At the same time, remember Paul's words to us when he felt weak and asked the Lord to remove the affliction:

But he said to me, "My grace is sufficient for you, for my power is made perfect in weakness." Therefore I will boast all the more gladly about my weaknesses, so that Christ's power may rest on me. (II Corinthians 12:9 NIV)

A significant challenge in life will help you see the truth. God's grace is not absent in such times; it is present in the trial. He is helping you see beyond yourself. He is helping you see the truth, hoping to set you free. Embrace the trial; embrace His love in it. Admit the truth. Be free.

Remember, I am not saying that you are not a chosen child of the King; you are. I am not saying that you are not created in His image and endowed with every good and perfect gift; you are. The problem is that we too often forget His role in our lives: that He alone is Lord over all and that everything is a gift from His hand (I Corinthians 4:7; James 1:17).

I am just encouraging you to come back to the truth that you know in your heart. Live in that truth and it will set you free.

CHAPTER THREE

The Scars of War

September 11

Good afternoon to my faithful prayer partners! I wanted to give you an update after my first week of radiation. All went very well and God's hand continues to strengthen and bless me. I can tell there is some additional fatigue every day and can only attribute that to the radiation. I cannot yet tell whether it will have an increasing or cumulative impact, but I guess we will find out this week! Otherwise I am still fortunate that about all I am experiencing is the fatigue from the chemo, typically hitting on Sunday and lasting into Monday.

On the learning front, I am reading a book titled <u>Affliction</u> by Edith Schaeffer. She looks at victory over affliction in the life of the Christian as being so much more than just beating the disease. Every time the afflicted believer says a prayer, gives a testimony of hope or simply worships the King as our healer, in the cosmic war between Heaven and Hell it hands Satan another defeat. So I will keep on praising, praying and giving testimony as long as I have breath!

You do the same!

In His Grace,

Steve

In my early years as a Christian, I felt that "the testing of your faith" mentioned in the first chapter of the Book of James meant that man was persecuting you for being a Christian. That can certainly be the case, but I have since learned that testing comes in many forms. Ultimately, it is Satan who persecutes us. He may use man, sickness, global economic failure or any number of things. But we also need to understand the scriptural truth that God allows this persecution in order to test and grow our faith. This testing is part of His plan. He both allows the test and at the same time makes available to us everything we need in order to pass it. Our task is to remain true to the reality of God's power and grace in our lives to see us through whatever challenge may come our way.

In her wonderful book *Affliction* (Fleming H. Revel, 1978), Edith Schaeffer reminds us that Satan wants to destroy anything that brings glory to God; if we are glorifying God, then Satan wants to destroy us. Schaeffer points to our praise during affliction as not only an act of faithful obedience, but a strike against God's enemies. We need to hold true to our faith *especially* in the midst of the storm and realize that we have victory when we praise God in the midst of a trial, even if the affliction ultimately destroys us in the process.

We are soldiers in the war between Heaven and Hell. War brings scars, both physical and emotional. Jesus has scars from the war; scars that bring strength, healing and ultimate victory to the soldiers of the King.

My own recent skirmish marred my skin with scars from spinal surgery and radiation. On my body, I literally bear marks that remind me of the reality of death. But, on my soul I also bear the kiss of a King; a King who has bought me with His blood and written my name in His Book of Life to show all creation that I am His. (See Philippians 4:3; Revelation 3:5, 20:15, 21:27.)

The scars of war will fade and pass, but the kiss of the King is <u>eternal</u>. Our hope is sure and His promises are not empty!

Rejoice in those promises, precious believer, and stay in the battle. Rejoice!

CHAPTER FOUR

The Intimate Voice of God

September 16

To my faithful prayer partners:

Sometimes God can communicate to us in ways that are so intimate that it is scary. I was walking through the hospital yesterday on the way to the parking garage after my morning radiation treatment. To get to the elevator from the radiation unit, I have to walk past my oncologist's office. As I passed, I said a little prayer, a big one actually, that the report from my blood work last Friday would be good news. On this road you always wonder if the chemo is actually working; you know what you are feeling, but you don't know what is actually happening.

Well, two minutes later I was getting into my car and I received a text from my oncologist. The blood tests showed that the M proteins, the "bad stuff" in my blood that indicates myeloma, have dropped by over 50%! I <u>unabashedly</u> share that I shed a tear or two there in my car. Only four weeks of chemo and I am 50% better... what a God we have! And *how tender of Him to give me the news just when I needed it and asked for it. This is not the first time, as you have read in my earlier emails. Still, I continue to be astounded that the God of the universe knows my name, where I am standing, what I am feeling... wow!*

I have made it through 8 out of 10 of my radiation treatments and today will mark the half-way point on my chemo treatments, based on original expectations. I have not lost sight of the fact that I am doing only my little part to achieve the results reflected above. Your prayers, constant encouragement and support are simply huge as I walk down this road. Thanks for walking with me... and keep it up!

Steve

I am obviously not the only one who has realized how intimate God can be:

Jesus saw Nathanael coming toward him and said of him, "Behold, an Israelite indeed, in whom there is no deceit!" Nathanael said to him, "How do you know me?" Jesus answered him, "Before Philip called you, when you were under the fig tree, <u>I saw you</u>." Nathanael answered him, "Rabbi, you are the Son of God! You are the King of Israel!" Jesus answered him, "Because I said to you, 'I saw you under the fig tree,' do you believe? You will see greater things than these." (John 1:47-50 ESV)

For you formed my inward parts;
you knitted me together in my mother's womb.
Your eyes saw my unformed substance;
in your book were written, every one of them,
the days that were formed for me,
when as yet there was none of them. (Psalm 139:13, 16 ESV)

I am often perplexed by the following question: How is it that the Great I Am, the Lord Almighty, the Holy God of Israel, would actually take any notice of me, the weak, the totally dependent, the wretched, the sinner?

Along my journey so far, I have experienced God's intimate response in several different and amazing ways. Can He really be this personal? Sure, there is a level of awe as to His omniscience; that He knows everything about everything from before time began to its very end. But even that is not the awe that I feel when I know He just heard me and that He just answered. This is not just a God who sits on a throne seeing all and knowing all, shrouded in glory and seemingly untouchable. This is a God who bends down to whisper in my ear that He just heard me!

In Psalm 139 David tells us that God knows each detail of our existence. He formed us. He knows us and He knows our days. Read the gospels and listen to the words of Jesus, who knows those details too. God came and dwelt among us as a man. He knows what we are feeling. He has felt it too. He knows the pain, the sorrow, and the fear that we feel.

Call to Him. He hears you. He is listening right now.

CHAPTER FIVE

Knowing Where You Are

September 27

All: You will never have any idea how important you are to me and how I take renewed strength every day from knowing that you and many others are praying for me. Let me get you focused on a couple of specific requests:

1. *Last Friday the number of my white blood cells had dropped, as had the subcomponents of those cells that actually fight infection. This is important since both those numbers need to stay at a certain level for me to continue to receive my weekly chemo treatment. I want to stay the course and not have to skip any rounds and prolong this ordeal. Again, all of this is in God's hands, but please join me in praying that my white blood cell counts and especially the counts for those sub-cells that fight infection would remain high and even return to their previous levels so that I can continue the fight.*

2. *I am beginning to feel what I expect are some cumulative effects of the chemo and radiation. The fatigue is more constant*

and my stomach is often just not right. I have also been fight-
ing some insomnia. Please pray that I can get my rest at night.

That is enough for me to ask for, but I also want you to do
something else for me. Simply praise God for who He is and
what He has done for all of us. If you are a believer in Jesus
and His sacrifice as the payment for your sins, your salvation
*is **secure**... praise God for that! No matter what may hap-*
pen here on earth, whether to your body, your finances, your
*job, whatever... your salvation is secure. And **even more** than*
that, although we are not promised absence of affliction, we
are promised that God is with us and will never forsake us;
we are promised a Comforter to walk beside us; we are prom-
ised a daily, waking, walking and communicating relation-
ship with the God of the universe who made us and loves us
and knows us individually. These are promises that overcome
trials— promises that stare affliction in the face, promises that
enable us to remain hopeful. Praise God for reaching down
and revealing Himself to us, so that we can know Him and
experience His pervasive, overwhelming love.

Resting in that love,

Steve

Do you feel that you are in God's hands when affliction comes your
way? No, I am not asking the basic theological question of whether God
is in complete control over the circumstances in our lives. (Even Satan and
his hordes admit that fact: see James 2:19.) What I am asking is whether
you feel safe in God's arms; whether you take comfort in that relationship.
I am asking what you feel in your heart, not what you think. If you read
Scripture, it is unquestionable that God is in control of all things. But,
how does your personal relationship with God make you feel when you are
in the midst of a trial? Yes, *especially* when you are in the midst of a trial.

Do you want to know how David felt? Look at Psalm 91 (highlights added):

He who dwells in the shelter of the Most High
will abide in the shadow of the Almighty.
I will say to the LORD, "My refuge and my fortress,
My God, in whom I trust!"
For it is He who delivers you *from the snare of the trapper*
and from the deadly pestilence.
He will cover you with His pinions,
and under His wings you may seek refuge;
His faithfulness is a shield and bulwark.

You will not be afraid *of the terror by night,*
or of the arrow that flies by day;
Of the pestilence that stalks in darkness,
or of the destruction that lays waste at noon.
A thousand may fall at your side
and ten thousand at your right hand,
But it shall not approach you.
You will only look on with your eyes
and see the recompense of the wicked.
For you have made the LORD, my refuge,
even the Most High, your dwelling place.
No evil will befall you,
nor will any plague come near your tent.

For He will give His angels charge concerning you,
to guard you in all your ways.
They will bear you up in their hands,
that you do not strike your foot against a stone.
You will tread upon the lion and cobra,
the young lion and the serpent you will trample down.
*"Because he has loved Me, therefore **I will deliver him**;*
***I will set him securely on high**, because he has known My name.*

*He will call upon Me, and **I will answer him**;*
***I will be with him** in trouble;*
***I will rescue him** and honor him.*

With a long life I will satisfy him
and let him see My salvation." (NASV)

Do you wish you had the confidence of David? Is the Lord your dwelling place, your refuge? Have you developed that level of personal relationship with an all-powerful God so that you do actually trust Him, that you can lean back and rest in His care, confident of His love for you?

To "dwell" is not a casual relationship. It is not a relationship that happens sporadically, simply spending a moment here and there or when you have time. You dwell in it. You stop, focus and pour your heart, soul and mind into it. Have you done that with God? Me neither. But I am trying harder at it. I am waking up every day, grabbing a big stick and fighting with renewed strength against those distractions that would keep me from pursuing the most important relationship in my existence. If I want to enjoy a relationship with God in the same way David did, then I need to make Him my refuge, my dwelling place. So do you.

Want some really good news? God created you and actually desires to have that level of relationship with you. (See I John 3:1; 4:9-10.) And no matter how many times you fail at this task, you can start again. God's patience and forgiveness are limitless and everlasting. (See Psalm 103:12; Romans 8:39.) Each time you start again, as I have done many times, begin by praising God for who He is and remember that your salvation is secure.

We have been offered an intimate, ongoing relationship with the God of the universe, but He will not force it on us. We need to step into it, not casually, but with intention. We must dwell in it, just like David did.

CHAPTER SIX

A New Shape

October 13

All: I delayed this update in hopes of having the results of my blood tests from the end of my second month of chemo. Those may not come until later in the week, so I decided not to delay any longer. Thank you for your faithful prayer support; pray with me that I will again get good results.

I will be facing a big decision in the coming weeks and would solicit your prayers for discernment and clear leading. I am considering whether to have a stem cell transplant, which is a process where the doctor takes stem cells from my blood and stores them before giving me a really heavy dose of chemo that (unfortunately) wipes out my immune system while it searches to destroy any remaining cancer. The protected stem cells are then reinserted into my bloodstream so that they begin to rebuild my immune system. Unfortunately, I need to stay in a sealed room for however long it takes for my immune system to get back to a safe level. Typically it takes two to three weeks. Even after that, you are encouraged to stay at home and not return to an office environment for three months.

As you can see, this is a huge step. Fortunately, with technology, I can do most of my work without needing to come to the office. Even in the sealed room I can handle about 90% of what I do. Still, there is a lot to consider. I look at it as "washing" the bone marrow to enhance the chance of staying in remission, especially when followed by maintenance drugs. Some oncologists feel that the quality and performance of the maintenance drugs have advanced over the last 5 years to the point where stem cell transplant therapy may no longer be necessary; hence my dilemma.

On the learning front, one morning I received two devotionals from unrelated sources. The unusual thing was that they were separate pieces on the same topic and by the same author! Here was the topic: the deep challenges of life and what to do when you are in them. One piece spoke of leaning on God and learning what He has for you. The other used the example of how a grand piano is made; a straight piece of wood is subjected to tremendous pressure over a period of time, enough to make sure that the wood remains in its new shape, never to return to its old shape again.

The most remarkable thing is that both of these devotionals showed up the morning after I prayed a prayer that I would not return to the same man I was before this experience, that I would not go back to the same things I was doing or have the same perspectives I had at that time. I wanted to remain at this place of newfound understanding of what is important, of how important it is to live each moment for the Kingdom and for things eternal, that will not rust and fade. I wanted God to ensure that I did not simply go back to my same "shape" before He blessed me with this trial… Do you think He heard me?

All praises to the God who is so personal and so ready to answer us when we call.

Steve

Paul tells us in Romans 8:29 that we have been chosen by God to be conformed to the image of Christ. For us, just as for a stubborn plank of wood, this takes time. God in His wisdom has ordained that we become like Christ through a work in our hearts of personal transformation. But it is a process, not an event. It is not as simple as flipping a switch.

Your salvation (justification) is an event that is sure and settled by the sacrifice of Christ for you, but the process of becoming holy (sanctification) takes time. Jesus learned through suffering (Hebrews 5:8) and so do we. His transformative work inside us, the cleansing, stretching, bending, washing... whatever you want to call it, is not the work of a moment, but of a lifetime.

So, when you are in the midst of your next unexpected detour, look for what God is trying to teach you. Listen for what He is saying to you through circumstances, through His Word and through those around you. Consider what He may be addressing in your life and why He is addressing it. God is there with you in the trial. Draw near to Him and experience His presence at a level you may never have known before. He will change your heart for the better. He will reshape you more into the image of His Son, Jesus. And He will do it in a way that will lessen the chance that you will go back to your old "shape" and the old habits that you had before the trial.

He is clearly reshaping me through my experience with cancer. I listen differently, I see differently and I interact differently with others. The Word of God is more important to me, my time with God is more treasured and people and relationships are more precious.

Such is the purpose of God-ordained challenges that we face in life; they test our hearts and our beliefs and change us in the process. Reflect on James 1:2-4. Ask God to work His desired purposes in your life and let your next trial have its intended effect.

CHAPTER SEVEN

Growing in Wisdom and Faith

October 23rd

All: I recently received the report from my second round tests and the cancer indicator dropped another 50%! Thanks again for your continued prayers on my behalf!

After considerable research into stem cell transplant therapy, here is the bottom line: a transplant will likely extend my period of remission. I wish it would do more; I wish it was a cure, but it is not. That said, if it will extend my remission, then it is a path that I will take, by God's grace.

I will not be going down that path immediately, however. God has built another 30 days into my journey. I have made great progress, with my cancer indicators dropping from 2.1 when we started to 1.1 a month later and now to .5 after two months. I am so thankful for God's answer to all of your prayers on my behalf, as well as my own. My oncologist feels that the indicators may not even be detectable by the end of this month! But since I am tolerating the chemo so well, he wants to do a 4th round in order to clean my bone marrow even further before my stem cell "harvest" takes place. A second oncologist we contacted agrees with that advice and it sounds like a good idea to me as well. Since the harvested stem cells will be the basis for my new immune system following the transplant, let's get them as clean as possible! This means that I will still be taking chemo through the end of November. Then the stem cell transplant process starts with 30 days of tests and pretreatments, with the actual procedure starting after that period. So the good news is that the timing will allow me to enjoy both the Thanksgiving and Christmas holidays. Praise God with me for that added blessing!

Honestly, I had hoped to avoid the transplant process, but wisdom and counsel guide me otherwise and God has given me a peace that He will certainly be with me through it. I had not planned on a 30-day extension of the chemo, but again wisdom and counsel both point me down that path. There are always unwanted or unexpected turns in the road; finding God's plan is the key. Your prayers on my behalf help guide me and I so appreciate your endurance. Please do not get discouraged (even if I do) and hang in there with me! John Ortberg has a great chapter in his book The Life You've Always Wanted (Zondervan, 1997) concerning spiritual disciplines. Chapter 12 is about endurance through an ordeal. He compares it to a marathon where the runner "hits the wall" and the body does not want to go another step. Ortberg says that every runner knows what they have to do at that point… they have to keep running.

Having you each beside me helps me keep running. I see hills up ahead, but a God who is bigger; much, much bigger.

Steve

The apostles grew in their faith by overcoming challenges. They endured ridicule, personal loss, floggings, false criminal charges, imprisonment, mob violence, and eventual martyrdom for the sake of the Gospel. Paul recounts his own sufferings at length in 2 Corinthians 11:24-28.

As we saw in an earlier chapter, even Jesus "grew" as a man in his relationship with God through trial. "Although he was a son, he learned obedience from what he suffered." (Hebrews 5:8 NIV) As He grew from a boy into a man, He grew in His human understanding of our trials by participating in them Himself.

If you and I ask to grow in wisdom, faith and the ability to serve God with a pure heart, how can He change our hearts and our character except through difficulties and testing? Some wisdom can be gained by reading and study, but most of it is learned experientially. Our faith can grow by hearing what God has done in the life of another, but we will grow even more by experiencing God's faithfulness in our own lives. Experiencing cancer and all that comes with it may be the best way that I can gain deeper wisdom and deeper faith to pass on to my family and others. If so, then I need to be okay with it. It is the same with you in your own particular trials.

Obtaining wisdom and faith is neither a quick process nor an easy one; it takes work. And it also often takes the experience of walking through really tough circumstances to set both deep within us. Remember, He promises to hold on to us through any trial and to never forsake us (Hebrews 13:5).

Trials are a necessary part of the sanctification process and they are part of the plan of a God who loves us; a plan that He established before the beginning of time. Christ grew through the trials in His life when He walked among us; we need to grow through our own trials so that we can become more like Him.

CHAPTER EIGHT

Don't Look at Statistics

November 5

Faithful friends: Thank you all for your prayers concerning my decision about where I would have my stem cell transplant procedure. Since I last updated you, I have researched facilities and staff, disease and treatment protocols, the number of cases handled at different facilities and treatment success rates.

Becky and I were able to tour a facility in Tampa yesterday. It is a beautiful facility with an excellent staff. As we listened for the Lord's voice, however, we did not see or hear anything that made us feel that He was leading us in that direction. We will be touring the facility in Orlando this Wednesday. The more we understand about the numerous appointments before the actual treatment, as well as the many follow-up appointments after the transplant, the more we realize how important being close to home will be. We are leaning strongly towards choosing the facility nearest to where we live, unless the Lord shows us something to turn us in another direction.

Good news from my last oncology appointment on Friday! I have one important reading that has already gone back to a normal level. I will get final numbers from the blood tests following the end of my third round of chemo next week and I will let you know how those came out. Thank you again so much for your prayers; they have gotten me to this point! Perhaps the best news I received yesterday is that I will only need three weeks of treatments this round; my last treatment will be November the 18th, which means no chemo through Thanksgiving and on through Christmas!

More next week!

Steve

As you've probably guessed before now, I like to do my homework. But when you go through as much internet research as I did, for example, to find the right transplant facility, you get more information than you really want. One chunk of that is mortality statistics. As you can imagine, especially with cancer, they are not very comforting.

In the midst of my discouragement, the Lord told me to remember one thing... He is not controlled by statistics. Statistics, by definition, look backwards and tell you what *has* happened. At best, they can only *predict* what is to come, but they *cannot dictate* it. Only God knows what is to come; only He controls the future. It is comforting to know the One who guides our steps and watches over us.

Did Joshua look at statistics before marching around Jericho? (Joshua 6)

Did Gideon consider the statistical improbability that only 300 men could rout the whole Midianite army? (Judges 7)

Did Peter think of the statistics before walking on water? (Matthew 14:28-29)

Of course they did; well, maybe not impulsive Peter. Regardless, these men trusted God and stepped out in faith. We should do the same.

God has given me peace that He is in control. He has not given me the assurance of another 20 years; the truth is that none of us has the certainty of even another day. The assurance I have is that He holds me in His hands right now and will throughout every day that I walk before Him. That assurance is all that is promised to us while He keeps us on this earth… and it is all we need.

So don't look at the statistical chances of making it through whatever trial you are facing. Immerse yourself in God's character, His faithfulness, His power and His love for you. *That* is knowledge that will sustain you.

CHAPTER NINE

Chasing After Wind

November 11

All: I wanted to share my joy with you that my recent blood tests showed no evidence of cancer! Rejoice! I could not have gotten this far without your love and prayers. We know the journey is continuing, so keep it up!

I have also made a final decision to have the stem cell transplant done here in Orlando. God has given Becky and me a great peace after our tour of the facility this week. One of my specific prayers was that we would be able to step inside a vacant room (a little rare) and we were able to do so. It helps me to have a mental picture of where I will be for several weeks. God then went even further ahead of my expectations by having the scheduling nurse prepare a tentative schedule for me! This was awesome because it allows me to plan my work schedule around a rather large number of December physicians' appointments before the January transplant procedure. For an obsessively detailed planner like me, this was a real gift! God is awesome in how He knows our needs and goes before us.

A devotional from Charles Spurgeon's <u>Morning and Evening</u> for November 9th looked at Colossians 2:6 and the concept of "walking" in Christ. His challenge to us is that we walk intentionally so that we <u>actually progress</u> in our faith. Sunday morning church attendance or a Bible reading every day may be less than the commitment we need. Spurgeon says: "...run forward until you reach the uttermost degree of knowledge that a man can attain concerning our Beloved." That is a high calling. Pick up the challenge with me and press on!

Steve

Before God blessed me with this unexpected detour (this is not tongue in cheek; see James 1), my typical pattern was to get up before 6, have my quiet time before the Lord, shower, shave, grab breakfast and be out the door before 7:30. I would leave the office around 6:15 or 6:30 that evening. Dinner by 7, then once a week there was a Bible study and typically on another night a meeting of some sort. There went two nights. On two other nights, at least in recent years now that the kids are up and gone, I would arrive home, throw on the workout gear and be "engaged" in some extreme fitness for an hour and a half before dinner. There went two more nights. Saturday morning was another workout followed by weekly yard chores, etc. (providing a good "cool down" to the workout). Office work often found its way into the weekend. This will sound familiar to many of you.

In a wonderful book called *How People Change* (New Growth Press, 2008), Paul Tripp and Tim Lane make this statement: "Quite simply, we worship what we find attractive." What do you find attractive? I obviously found work attractive, or at least the fruits of work. I also found the benefits of exercise attractive. I can rationalize all day long about why I was pursuing both. At least in part, if I am honest with myself, I was "chasing after wind" as the Teacher cries out in the book of Ecclesiastes. Was I being a good steward of my time and talents, telling myself that I was "making money for the Kingdom"? Whose kingdom was I building? Was I taking care of my body as the temple of the Holy Spirit? Or was I chasing after something that I thought would make my life better, something that I felt was essential to my happiness? Was my identity wrapped up in these things? Were they the seat of my security?

We do not talk enough about idols. No, not the hand-carved little rock images placed on a shelf and surrounded by candles; we are much too sophisticated for that. We carve our idols on the pages of fitness or glamour magazines, or on our bank books and retirement portfolios. I cannot tell you about your heart, but I can see some things I do not like in my own: things that have been mercifully revealed to me through this ordeal by a loving Father. I was putting too much trust in fitness to prolong my life. I was working really hard to continue to stack up assets as a shelter. Ecclesiastes 7:12 tells me money can be a shelter, just as wisdom can be; the difference is that wisdom can save your life, and money cannot. The number of hours that I spent chasing money clearly eclipsed the hours spent in pursuing God's wisdom.

How attractive do you find Christ to be? How many hours a day do you pursue Him? How many hours a day do you spend "pursuing" other things that you find attractive? Add them up. It will tell you a lot about your heart and the idols you are chasing.

CHAPTER TEN

Death, Renewal and Hope

November 18

My friends: Today is scheduled as my final day of chemo. This is a good day! I got up and took what I hope will be the last thirteen pills of one weekly chemo medication. An hour later, I took what I hope will be the last ten pills of another one. I just left the oncologist's office having received what I hope will be my last weekly injection of a third chemo drug. This is a good day! I know in God's providence that the way forward may be different than I anticipate, but I can rejoice in the hope that I will not be at this place again. And if I ever am, I can rejoice that the same loving God who got me through this so far will be right beside me again. This is a good day!

In my devotions recently I read II Corinthians 4:16: "Therefore we do not lose heart, but though our outer man is decaying, yet our inner man is being renewed day by day." (NASV) I understand this verse now more than I ever did in the past. Life is all about death and renewal. We have to die to ourselves in order to live for Christ. We see every form of life around us grow and die; it is inescapable. Yet even as we watch ourselves grow older, we know that His spirit is sanctifying our hearts as we lean into Him for our very breath. It is His ordained pattern, showing us in death the penalty of sin's coming into the world, but showing too that there is yet the hope of coming glory as He changes our hearts before our very eyes!

I love you all. Thank you so much for your prayers. Have a great Thanksgiving next week!

In His Peace,

Steve

Our hope is in what is eternal. Paul tells us in II Corinthians why we should have hope: "For our light and momentary troubles are achieving for us an eternal glory that far outweighs them all. So we fix our eyes not on what is seen, but on what is unseen, since what is seen is temporary, but what is unseen is eternal." (4:17-18 NIV)

Earlier in the same passage, Paul reminds us that we carry this hope, this expectation of something wonderful, in jars of clay: vessels that are fragile and exposed to the overwhelming risks of life. He relates how on different occasions he had been hard pressed, perplexed, persecuted and struck down. The only way that he could describe these afflictions as "light and momentary troubles" is that he was focused on something other than the affliction. He was focused on the prize of eternal glory.

In the physical world we see the cycle of death and renewal all around us. We see the acorn fall from the tree, lying lifeless on the ground, but eventually becoming a towering oak. We see death coming with hard winters, only to be followed by the glory of spring. For as long as time continues, the physical world can rest in the hope of spring following winter.

In the spiritual world, we carry something much more incredible than a recurring spring: we carry the *gospel*, the hope of *eternal* glory. Sin brings death, the Spirit of the Living God brings life, and salvation promises us eternal glory! The gospel calls us to die to sin and live for Christ every day, so that we gain that eternal promise. Paul gives us deeper insight into this perspective:

> *But whatever were gains to me I now consider loss for the sake of Christ. What is more, I consider everything a loss because of the surpassing worth of knowing Christ Jesus my Lord, for whose sake I have lost all things. I consider them garbage, that I may gain Christ and be found in him, not having a righteousness of my own that comes from the law, but that which is through faith in Christ — the righteousness that comes from God on the basis of faith. I want to know Christ — yes, to know the power of his resurrection and participation in his sufferings, becoming like him in his death, and so, somehow, attaining to the resurrection from the dead.*

> *Not that I have already obtained all this, or have already arrived at my goal, but I press on to take hold of that for which Christ Jesus took hold of me. Brothers and sisters, I do not consider myself yet to have taken hold of it. But one thing I do: Forgetting what is behind and straining toward what is ahead, I press on toward the goal to win the prize for which God has called me heavenward in Christ Jesus.* (Philippians 3:7-14 NIV)

When your "outer man" is being pummeled by trial and your "inner man" needs renewal, do what Paul did. Fix your eyes on what is eternal, not on what is temporary. Your journey may take a hundred different turns, but the eternal promise of coming glory remains unchanged.

Take the attitude attributed to our Saviour as your example: "Let us fix our eyes on Jesus, the author and perfecter of our faith, who for the joy set before him endured the cross, scorning its shame, and sat down at the right hand of the throne of God." (Hebrews 12:2 NIV)

CHAPTER ELEVEN

God Is Bigger

December 16

After numerous tests last week and this week, I had a successful surgery yesterday to insert my tri-catheter line. This is a small tube with three ends through which blood can be drawn and multiple medications administered. The line will be used to harvest the stem cells in December and to administer my chemo and any other necessary drugs, transfusions, etc. in January as part of the transplant. I know it avoids a large number of needle stabs that would otherwise be necessary, but you should see this thing! One line coming out from under my skin that then splits into three lines, each with a shut off valve and a different colored cap… I thought one of them would surely be a USB connector! Praise God for the wisdom He has given man to do such amazing things! Next Tuesday, I will be spending 6 hours in a recliner having the stem cells harvested. Pray that the doctor gets all the cells he needs on Tuesday, so that I do not have to repeat the process on Wednesday.

I did not even add to my last update that another close member of the family was having a heart catheterization on Tuesday; you can say a prayer for that recovery as well. Yes, we are weathering some storms, but God is greater than what we face and we are learning that more and more. I said to a dear friend who I know is praying for me, "If your God is not big enough to handle what life is throwing at you, then you have the wrong God!" Mine is big enough! Is yours? Sometimes I think we limit God and make Him small in our eyes, thinking He may not be big enough to listen or big enough to act. At least that is what we suggest when we try to control things and solve problems in our own way. It is certainly what our fears suggest.

Remember, especially during this season, that He does love you, He does listen and He does act. He is big enough. See Him that way, even lying in a Manger.

Steve

"God is bigger than _____." No matter what you use to fill in the blank, God is still bigger. He is simply staggering, beyond our comprehension. Words are inadequate to describe Him. The best we can find are those that He used when He spoke to Moses: He said His name was "I Am" (Exodus 3:14). How much bigger can you get? He never sleeps. He sees everything. His arm is neither short nor weak. His timing is always perfect. His actions are beyond question. He makes promises and keeps them without fail. Every gift that has been given to us comes from Him (James 1:17). We cannot draw a breath and our hearts cannot beat, except by His grace.

Before my diagnosis, I knew God was big. He became even bigger when I had to face cancer. Everything else got smaller; everything on my calendar, everything that I was chasing, and everything that I was striving to achieve — it all became very small. But this is as it should be. We need Him to get bigger when we face what seems overwhelming. We need to know that He is stronger than we thought and that He is completely faithful and trustworthy.

Most important, we need to know that His love for us is bigger than we ever thought it was: His love, His power, His faithfulness are our only comforts when we are in the midst of a trial. Our hope will not be in our own strength. If we could solve it with our own strength, then it would not be much of a trial.

How big is your God? If He is not big enough to handle every conceivable thing that life can throw at you, maybe you have the wrong God. Or, at least, maybe you have the wrong view of God. If your view of God is that He can only handle the small things, then your view needs to change. And be careful here — if your view of God is that He only handles the big things and you handle the small stuff, then your view still needs to change. If God is in complete control, then He handles it all and we need to acknowledge that, trusting Him with every detail of our lives.

My God is big enough. My God is the Lord Jehovah, maker of heaven and earth, the Great I Am! I know that He is sovereign; I know that He is able and I know that He loves me. He has never failed me in the past, He will not fail me now, nor will He fail me in the future, whatever it holds for me.

CHAPTER TWELVE

The Word "Through"

January 1

I hope that all of you had a wonderful Christmas and New Year holiday with your families, enjoying God's rich blessings. I sure did! We had a great time spending Christmas with my granddaughter (except for the cold someone "blessed" me with!).

I should be entering the transplant unit this Wednesday the 4th. I say "should" since the process is that you pack your bag and then wait for the phone call confirming that a bed is coming available. If so, you need to be there in an hour to make sure you do not lose it to another patient. Sometimes demand from other areas of the hospital will force an overflow into the unit, so you have to be nimble! Of course, there is also the possibility that all beds remain occupied longer than expected, since the immune system needs to return to a certain level before a patient can safely be released from isolation. There is also the (I hope slight) chance that they will delay my admission when I tell them I picked up a cold over Christmas. From my perspective it is almost gone, but when someone is about to intentionally destroy your immune system, they may feel differently. Yes, pray for wisdom for my doctors on making that call.

Where am I in my prayers? Continuing remission for decades; few if any side effects from the chemo; an ability to witness to every one of my care givers and other patients if the opportunity arises; protection for my dear wife as she walks through this with me. I know you are standing with me in these prayers, and I continue to appreciate your faithfulness.

I was having lunch with two long-term business associates a week or so ago and giving them the details of my story, only some of which they knew. One of them looked at me and asked, "How in the world do you keep such a positive attitude?" Before I could respond, the other associate turned to him and said, "His life is in the hands of Christ and he's obviously okay with that!" I could not have said it better. As one who has been trying to quietly witness to others through the years concerning God's faithfulness, this was very encouraging. God be praised.

So my next update will likely come from my room at the transplant center. I have told others that part of me looks forward to three weeks of close fellowship with God, listening to what He has to say to me. After all, a forced period of separation from normalcy can often open your ears. The other part of me wonders if I am about to enter into the ring with an adversary who, even if I leave victorious, will certainly pummel me physically. Regardless, I know God walks with me. His rod and His staff really are comforting. I guess it takes walking through a valley to make that clear.

Bring on the valley…

Steve

Psalm 23 has always been a source of hope and comfort to the believer. I obviously went to it quickly after my diagnosis. And, for the life of me, I cannot remember whether I simply saw it differently or whether I had heard it mentioned somewhere, but one word leapt off the page at me. A simple word in verse 4 that I had never focused on before. It was the word "through":

> *Even though I walk through the valley of the shadow of death,*
> *I will fear no evil, for You are with me;*
> *Your rod and Your staff, they comfort me. (ESV)*

David could have said "though I *fall into*" or "though I *cannot escape from*" the valley of death, but he didn't. David knew many valleys in his life, and God led him "through" each one. What a different thought it would have been if David had said "Although I am trapped in this valley of death, waiting for my end to come, I will fear no evil, for you are with me."

David was not talking about being comforted in death, but in life! I can certainly take solace in knowing that the great Comforter will be with me when my time on earth comes to an end. But as I continue on this journey, I take even more comfort from knowing that my Deliverer is walking me *through* this valley of affliction to the other side! It makes it easier for me to look at this trial and the next trial to come (and it will). These words give me hope that I will make it to the other side; they promise that I will be comforted all along the way by His rod and His staff.

I know a little more, now, about that walk. I know the comfort of that rod and staff. In the valley, these are not just words, the rod and the staff; they are tangible. The rod protects you from the enemy. The staff guides you as you walk. You can reach out and hold the staff even as He holds it. You can feel it as it moves, pace by pace. You know you are making it through to the other side. You know that you do not walk alone. Remember, He promises that His grace will be sufficient (II Corinthians 12:9).

Charles Spurgeon tells us: "There are seas of suffering that the sufferer must navigate alone. No other sail is in sight. Scan the horizon and nothing is seen but wave after wave. Now is your hour for faith in the great Lord, who holds even lonely seas in the hollow of His hand (Isaiah 40:12)." (*Beside Still Waters*, Thomas Nelson, 1999, p.11)

This is the way of trial and testing. Reach out and take hold of Him. Have no fear, He will get you through.

CHAPTER THIRTEEN

Waiting In The Desert

January 3

All: My doctor is concerned that my cold from Christmas has lingered and he does not want to hit me with the chemo and knock out my immune system until he feels completely sure all traces of the cold are gone. So my admission date has been postponed a week. I know it is good to be conservative, but this is hard to take emotionally. I was ready to get on and get it over with, but obviously God has other plans.

So it will be business as usual for the next week. Pray that the Z pack that I am going to pick up shortly works really well!

Thanks again for your prayers and faithfulness!

Steve

Jan 6th

All: I am still in waiting mode. The initial shock of having to delay my transplant for a week wore off after a day.

Thanks to many of you who gently reminded me that God controls all things in the life of the believer (Romans 8:28), including the timing of my transplant! I had to remember that waiting patiently is part of the Christian pilgrimage. Here I was, failing to trust God with my admission date, when at the same time I said that I trusted Him with the much more amazing mystery of designing stem cells to engraft into bone marrow. Another example of how I often trust Him with the big things, but not the small ones, especially when I am impatient.

So, if God wishes it so in His timing, I will enter the transplant unit Wednesday. That will only occur after I have a chest x-ray and a doctor visit to see if I am "all clear" to go forward. Please pray for that success with me. Most importantly, however, pray that God moves me into the unit in His perfect timing, regardless of any schedule I have set in my heart. Then pray that I will hear Him during that period of relative solitude. Pray that you can hear Him too, even without going into the desert.

Steve

There I was, eager to get on with the transplant. God had other ideas, though, and delayed my entry into the hospital by a week because of a Christmas cold that still lingered. Initially, I was really upset that my idea of "perfect timing" was not going to happen.

I was having a hard time waiting. A great friend sent me this note as I lamented the delay:

Waiting can be difficult. It often causes us to think the Lord is not in control as we wait. But God is worth waiting for. God uses waiting to refresh, renew and teach us. Make good use of your waiting times by discovering what God is trying to teach you in them.

Lamentations 3:24 – "The Lord is my portion; therefore I will wait for Him."
Psalms 37:7 – "Be still before the Lord and wait patiently for Him."
Psalms 40:1 – "I waited patiently for the Lord; He turned to me and heard my cry."

Often blessings cannot be received unless we go through the "trial of waiting". We need to ask God to help us find the balance between urgency and waiting; finding that optimum point of being diligent, being trusting and being surrendered.

These were words of wisdom that I needed to hear. Waiting under most circumstances is difficult, but waiting in the desert, where things are hard and God remains silent, can be really tough. We want so desperately to get across to the other side; to finish the test and have it behind us. But waiting is important, perhaps especially in the desert.

Os Hillman writes about such seasons in our lives: "In the desert God changes us and removes things that hinder us. He forces us to draw deep upon His grace. The desert is only a season in our life. When He has accomplished what He wants in our lives in the desert, He will bring us out. He has given us a mission to fulfill that can only be fulfilled after we have spent adequate time in preparation in the desert. Fear not the desert, for it is here you will hear God's voice like never before. It is here you become His bride. It is here you will have the idols of your life removed. It is here you begin to experience the reality of a living God like never before."

Remember that God controls not only the trial, but also the timing in it. Cry out to Him. He hears you and He will answer you (Isaiah 30:19-20). Wait patiently, as best you can, to hear His voice.

CHAPTER FOURTEEN

Why We Need Trials

January 10

All: I received a solid green light to go into the transplant process tomorrow!! Thank you so much for your prayers that helped make this possible! The Z pack did its thing and the chest x-ray was "beautiful" in the words of my doctor; he set me up to be admitted tomorrow.

So, what should you pray for now that this next step has started? How about this:

- *That admission goes smoothly so they can get the chemo administered before evening (which they tell me is preferable)*

- *That my body withstands the negative impacts of the chemo (not everyone reacts the same)*

- *That the reinsertion of my stem cells Friday goes smoothly and that they begin to engraft into my bone marrow as intended*

- *That I remain focused on Him and the opportunities He gives me to learn and even to minister to others who come into my world while there.*

That will be enough for now! Yes, you will be hearing from me further as I try to bring you along with me. On these journeys, we never know what might be around the corner... it is so comforting to know you are with me as brothers and sisters who care for me and lift me up! I will share what He shows me along the way, knowing that it is not meant for me alone, but for all of us as we seek to grow closer to Him.

*I will leave you with a great thought from Charles Spurgeon's <u>Morning and Evening</u> January 7 devotion. He says that we should be like a bull, standing between the plough and the altar, willing to work or to be sacrificed... **ready** for either. Chew on that when you start down your next unexpected path! The only way to even begin to rest in the journey is to trust the One who leads us, step by step. I trust Him... do you? I pray that you will, wherever life takes you.*

Steve

There can be no doubt that God uses challenges in our lives to teach us. He teaches us about Himself. He reveals His power by controlling the uncontrollable, His mercy by forgiving what seems unforgivable, or His miraculous ability to comfort us by relieving pain that we thought would last forever. But why does He need to use trials to get our attention and focus? David gives us insight in Psalm 119 on God's use of "afflictions" in his life to teach him the benefits of obeying God's decrees:

> *Teach me knowledge and good judgment,*
> *for I believe in your commands.*
> *Before I was afflicted I went astray,*
> *but now I obey your word.*
> *You are good and what you do is good;*
> *teach me your decrees.*

It was good for me to be afflicted,
So that I might learn your decrees.

I know, O LORD, that your laws are righteous,
and in faithfulness you have afflicted me. (vv. 66-68, 71, and 75 NIV)

At several points throughout this psalm, David laments that he has fallen away from being obedient. He knows that in order to live a pure life, he must obey God's commands. Yet he finds himself failing just as we do. Even in the very last verse of the psalm, David says that he has "strayed like a lost sheep." Do you ever feel that way? In John 14:15 and 23 Jesus tells us that if we love Him, we will obey Him. The choice before us and David is the same: will we obey the loving commands of a holy God?

In our natural state, we will not voluntarily discipline ourselves to take the necessary time and effort to learn God's laws and develop our relationship with Him at a deeper level. That kind of "pressing in" takes a lot of work. God can (and does) allow affliction in our lives to cause us to reach for Him, cling tighter to Him and dig deeper into that relationship.

This is how we grow. If He did not love us, he would not care about our growth. But He does care. In His love He will allow trials and afflictions, just as we sometimes need to use "tough love" with our own children to make sure they learn lessons that will protect and guide them later in life. He is a loving father to us and does the same, but with even more wisdom and more tenderness. We would never abandon our children in the midst of a tough-love trial; neither will He abandon us. He is not absent in our trials; He is very, very much present.

When affliction comes, remember the words of David above. Instead of running from it, try instead to hear what God is saying to you in the midst of it. He is your loving father and He is speaking to you. Listen hard. Press into Him for all you are worth! He wants you to be perfect and complete, lacking in nothing (James 1:4). Learn from the trial and then praise Him for loving you so much that He would take you through it.

Trials are tough, but they make us more like Jesus.

CHAPTER FIFTEEN

Listen for His Voice

January 14

All: My stem cells were reinserted successfully yesterday morning. There were about three or four pre-medications, one of which was a heavy dose of Benadryl. I had a great nap during the afternoon!

Now I am in the waiting stage to see what side effects may come over the next weeks. They tell me this is the hardest part, the waiting. It is especially hard if bad side effects from the chemo show up. All of them can be countered with medications, but you are still suffering through it. So here are the prayer requests:

- *That the chemo will do its intended work to rid my body of the cancer cells "hiding in the bushes" of my bone marrow;*

- *That my body will tolerate the chemo and that the side effects will be minimal at worst, or even not occur at all; and*

- *That the stem cells will do their job quickly, engrafting into the clean bone marrow to restart my immune system.*

I lift these prayers up to the Lord, who I know hears me. I understand how the prophet Habakkuk felt when he wrote "I will stand at my watch and station myself on the ramparts; I will look to see what He will say to me...." (Habakkuk 2:1 NIV)

Waiting is hard, but it is the waiting that makes us listen more diligently. I want to learn what He has for me here in this circumstance.

Thanks again for your prayers. I tell the nurses of your faithful prayers for me and they tell me they work! Keep it up!

Steve

Have you ever been at that place where you desperately wanted to hear God, to know that He was there for certain? Habakkuk knew that place of waiting. He had seen a great deal of injustice, strife and violence and he wanted to know what God was going to do about it. He cried out to God. And then he waited.

I lay in the isolation ward after my stem cell transplant, waiting to see what would happen. But I was also waiting on more than the passage of time, more than improving blood counts. I wanted to hear what God would say to me in the coming weeks, alone in that room. The desert has a purpose and I did not want to miss it.

Listening is a part of everyday life. Listening to a friend tell about their day requires one level of intensity. Listening to your boss at work requires a different level. But being alone, waiting and listening for the voice of God, is another thing altogether. We listen by looking at our circumstances as being ordained by God. We listen by looking diligently into His Word, working it deep into our hearts and minds and asking the Holy Spirit to show us how it applies to our situation. We also listen by sharing our requests with trusted friends who also listen to God, knowing that He may speak to us through them. God speaks through His Word, the circumstances that He orchestrates in our lives, the voices of others, and the still, quiet voice of His Spirit that speaks to our hearts.

David has comforting words in Psalm 121:1-2 for those who wait to hear God. The psalmist lifts his eyes to the hills, knowing that his help comes from the Lord, the maker of Heaven and earth. It is an incredible comfort to know that God hears us and wants to speak to us. But you do not need to wait for a desert experience to hear Him. God may use a challenge or an affliction to get your attention, as He did for me, but He can speak to you in a quieter voice: "Be still and know that I am God." (Psalm 46:10 ESV)

Are you taking the time to listen? There is no need to wait for a trial. Make time to be still and quiet, silencing all the distractions. Wait expectantly to hear His voice. Stay in His Word. Stay in fellowship. Look with a fresh perspective at your circumstances, and ask if God is speaking to you through them.

Jesus said, "My sheep listen to my voice; I know them and they follow Me." (John 10:27 NIV)

Listen for His voice.

CHAPTER SIXTEEN

Work Through It

January 16

All: Thanks so much for the faithful prayer support, without which I would not be up for this task. This is one of the hardest things I have ever done. Feeling the impacts of the chemo in my system, being checked every four hours around the clock, and being confined to this one room and the hallway outside got to me on Saturday, and I was understandably down. But many of you came to my rescue with great verses for me to claim and hold onto; and then God spoke further. One dear friend (in response to the last update) sent me Isaiah 30:19-20:

"For a people shall dwell in Zion, in Jerusalem; you shall weep no more. He will surely be gracious to you at the sound of your cry. ***As soon as he hears it, he answers you.*** *And though the Lord give you the bread of adversity and the water of affliction, yet your Teacher will not hide himself anymore, but* ***your eyes shall see your Teacher.****"*

This gave me great hope that God hears us the moment we cry out to him. Then God spoke to me through a devotional I received. The message was that when we are faced with adversity, we need to keep at the work that God has given us at the moment. By pursuing His work we pull ourselves above our circumstances and continue to look to the needs of others and to the Kingdom work God has called us to do.

So I committed to look at this room as my platform for the next several weeks, seeking opportunities to share my testimony of God's faithfulness. I had a nurse share with me last evening that she has a six-month-old son. I told her about my granddaughter of only five months and how God had miraculously brought her into this world through an emergency C-section the night before my spine surgery. I told her about her eye surgery at only four months of age and God's faithfulness in providing an incredible specialist and great success in the surgery.

God had impressed upon me, even before I came into the unit, that I should write down the story of my surgery and my granddaughter's birth, so that I could share what God had done for both of us. I gave this nurse a copy and she said that she would read it. Pray for the impact. God may be at work!!

My prayer requests remain the same as earlier. None of the bad side effects have shown up, only a little nausea this morning. Thank you Lord! Please also pray that I may use this platform as a faithful servant who has experienced God's mercy.

Thanks

Steve

When we are faced with a trial, our initial response is often to stop and drop everything so that we can focus all of our energy on this one thing. We want it to end. We want to know why it is happening and what we can do about it. "Business as usual" seems to be out of the question, if not impossible.

At one of my lowest points in the transplant recovery, God said something to me that I did not expect. He told me plainly to keep at whatever tasks He called me to, even in the midst of exhaustion, mind-numbing isolation and discouragement. He did not want me to simply be self-centered, focusing solely on what my body was going through; He wanted me to be "other centered." So — what did I have to work with? I had a small room and a few hallways attached to it. I also had a constant string of nurses, technicians and other staff who appeared every four hours around the clock, sometimes even more frequently. I began to write down all of their names. I had a platform, I had an audience and I had Jesus. All I needed to do was pray for opportunities and remain ready to walk into them as they were presented. It was really pretty awesome! And you know what else? It got my mind off of my circumstances and onto ministry and the work of the Kingdom. (See also Philippians 1:12, where Paul says his being in chains was actually advancing the gospel.)

A verse I had read many times began to make new sense to me:

> *Those who sow in tears*
> *will reap with songs of joy.*
> *He who goes out weeping,*
> *carrying seed to sow,*
> *will return with songs of joy,*
> *carrying sheaves with him. (Psalm 126:5-6 NIV)*

I had never before grasped the concept of sowing in tears. People in tears are suffering, rarely interested in anything but finding the source of the pain or how to ease it. Sowing implies giving, casting seeds so that good things spring forth; an unnatural thought for someone who is suffering. But God often calls us to do what seems for the moment unnatural, even radical; He was calling me to sow.

In the midst of affliction, in the midst of your tears, sow seeds for the Kingdom. Remain faithful and stay focused on the needs of others. God knows your own needs perfectly well. Even as He works to meet them in ways you struggle to see or understand, He still has work for you to do. It may even be that He can use you *especially* in the midst of your particular circumstances. You do not know who is watching and listening as you endure faithfully whatever God has allowed into your life. They may be going through a trying time and just need to hear someone say that God knows their needs, too. Be that someone.

Reaching out to another person while you yourself are struggling can be a powerful witness. Pray and look for opportunity. Stay at the work of the King. Look for the harvest and carry in sheaves with songs of joy. Reflect on Psalm 126 again. Sow seeds for the Kingdom even in the midst of your struggle. Show those around you that God is bigger than your trial, and that He is bigger than their trial, too.

CHAPTER SEVENTEEN

The Pace of Life

January 19

All: Well, the journey continues! Great news: as intended, the chemo has wiped out my old immune system! My white counts zeroed out this morning, meaning that I am in this danger zone of having no immune system at all… makes you lean on God's promises a little more! Any little "bug" that would just bounce off of you could stick to me and be an issue. They are hyper-clean here for good reason, so I have little concern. It should be another day or so of feeling completely wiped out as I do now, and then the new stem cells should begin to "reboot" the immune system and start me on an upward trajectory.

Thank you so much for your continuing prayers. I have not had any of the dreaded mouth sores that often accompany this process, praise God. Yesterday started with nausea and then everything hit my digestive system; it was a rough day and evening. God was still gracious through it all and the meds that they are giving me are taking the edge off. This is a commitment to a process, and you just have to know that going in. I feel like I am approaching the crest of the hill and that I will soon be looking down at the finish line! I feel the power of your prayers lifting my spirits and am blessed to have family with me many hours during the day. Although staff changes every 12 hours, I have even been able to develop some relationships that make this experience better.

This time of quietness has also had its precious moments every day. Listening to God in virtual solitude for hours at a time is incredible! I only hope that I can remember this after I am back home.

Thanks again for your constant prayers!

Steve

During one quiet moment in the transplant unit, God was speaking to me about "pushing" as opposed to "flowing" as we travel through life. There is a pace of life, a speed if you will, that allows life to feel more like a flow ordained by God and less like we are pushing ourselves to the limits every moment. We do not think very much about pacing ourselves in life, especially in America. Slowing the pace is simply not a big part of our culture. Even if you grew up in a small town which might have had at a slower pace, everything in the media and in the bigger cities around you would try to convince you that you need to speed up. American life, even in the church, defines success as pushing 100 hours of activity into 50. We jokingly lament that we do not "stop to smell the roses." Historically, it was not always this way. But the pace of life has increased over time and the speed seems to accelerate ever faster in our high-tech world.

Contrast what "flow" might look like. Think of how God led the Israelites in the desert. Look at Exodus 13:21-22:

By day the Lord went ahead of them in a pillar of cloud to guide them on their way and by night in a pillar of fire to give them light, so that they could travel by day or night. Neither the pillar of cloud by day nor the pillar of fire by night left its place in front of the people. (NIV)

When the cloud lifted, they moved, and not before. When the cloud settled, they stopped. It was a relationship of moment-by-moment watching and dependence. We, in contrast, run through life at a frantic pace, only now and then (often in times of crisis) taking time to look around to see if there even is a cloud anywhere in sight.

What would it look like if you pursued something only when you knew God was directing you to do so? What if God told you to rest more and pursue less… could you do it?

We need to have the discipline of attentive solitude if we expect to hear God in the daily and (even importantly) the major decisions in our lives. We need to take personal retreats, free from the normal, daily distractions in our lives, so that we can actually listen to a God who loves us, who has the direction we seek and who waits patiently to guide us. If you want a model, look at Jesus and how he cherished His own solitude before God. (See Matthew 4:1-11; 14:13, 23; 26:36-46; Mark 1:35; 6:31; Luke 6:12; 15:16.)

If you are not listening for God's voice, you certainly will not hear it.

We need to be still enough to listen; still enough to *hear*. How can you begin to build this into your life? I am asking myself the same question. Think on it. Listen. Be still. Recognize how imperative it is for you, for your family and those you touch that you are able to hear God speak.

"Be still, and know that I am God;
I will be exalted among the nations,
I will be exalted in the earth." (Psalm 46:10 NIV)

If we take the time to hear God, we will flow more and push less. Imagine a pace of life where you flow with God's specific will for your life. He has that plan, you know – that plan for you.

Don't you want to find it? Slow down and listen. Slow down and connect. Remember the words of Solomon, counted the wisest of men:

In vain you rise early
and stay up late,
toiling for food to eat—
for he grants sleep to those he loves. (Psalm 127:2 NIV)

CHAPTER EIGHTEEN

Bearing the Image

January 23

*Happy Monday everyone: I had one more really rough day
since my last update, but God stood there right beside me and
saw me through it. His strength continues to lift me daily. My
numbers are still very low, only slightly higher than bottom.
Pray for those stem cells! I need them to kick into gear and
propel me home. All in God's timing, not mine.*

*I have learned so much while I have been here. I have so much
more empathy for the invalid, shut-in and elderly who have
a limited ability to interact with the fast-paced world around
them. My room overlooks the two lakes adjacent to the East
side of the hospital, split by a major commuter highway. I see
hundreds of cars passing every day. Passing me by, not knowing that I am even here. I can imagine the pain felt by a
shut-in or a widow who isolates herself for years after losing a
spouse. Life could begin to lose meaning very quickly.*

*Our God is relational; He works through people more than
any other instrument. If you know someone who is isolated,*

you need to reach out to them. You may be the only one who does that day. Yes, it takes time, but you are literally extending life to them by showing them that you care enough to enter into their world.

We bear the image of Christ. When we extend His love, others see Him in us.

I love you all deeply. Thank you again so much for your prayers that continue to sustain me.

Steve

Did you get that? We bear the image of Christ and we are called to take that image into a dying world. Have you ever thought about what it really means and what it actually looks like in real life?

Read slowly and carefully through Philippians 2:6-8 as Paul talks about Jesus:

> *Who, being in very nature God,*
> *did not consider equality with God something to be grasped;*
> *but made himself nothing,*
> *taking the very nature of a servant,*
> *being made in human likeness.*
> *And being found in appearance as a man,*
> *he humbled himself*
> *and became obedient to death—*
> *even death on a cross! (NIV)*

Paul tells us that Christ, the second person of the Trinity, "was in the very nature God," which means that He had every attribute that God has, including limitless power and authority over all of creation. Yet He gave every bit of it up out of sheer love for us. He left it all to enter our world, heal our pain, and save us.

Do I do that? God has given me power, resources, time, and influence, but yet I often keep them to myself, for my own benefit. Is that reflecting His image?

No.

His image is one of sacrifice, spending His power on us and for our benefit. Are we doing the same? Do we hold back resources, or are we willing to sacrifice them for others, simply so that they see Christ in us? This is both the cost and high privilege of reflecting Christ. I need to grow here; too often I act as if His resources are limited and I need to retain what I have for me and my family. I act as if I have forgotten His promise to open the windows of heaven for us (Malachi 3:9-10)? I need to trust that He will take care of me and those I love even as I give away what He has placed into my hands as His steward.

I grasp too tightly. If you do, too, maybe we both need to believe — really believe — His promises:

I was young and now I am old,
yet I have never seen the righteous forsaken
or their children begging bread. (Psalm 37:25 NIV)

"Therefore everyone who hears these words of mine and puts them into
practice is like a wise man who built his house on the rock. The rain came
down, the streams rose, and the winds blew and beat against that house;
yet it did not fall, because it had its foundation on the rock." (Matthew
7:24-25 NIV)

"The second [great commandment] is this: 'Love your neighbor as yourself...'"
(Mark 12:31 NIV)

One man gives freely, yet gains even more;
another withholds unduly, but comes to poverty.
A generous man will prosper;
he who refreshes others will himself be refreshed.
(Proverbs 11:24-25 NIV)

Am I reflecting His image to my neighbor? Could I be convicted of following Christ by my actions in the world around me? Yes, many who are close to me and know my heart know that I love Christ. But what about those who do not know me well, those who only see my actions... would they see Christ in me?

Would they see Christ in you?

CHAPTER NINETEEN

Desiring Normal

January 27

All: I have been waiting daily to be released and to give you that good news. God has not ordained that yet, so I wanted to give you an update. My numbers are climbing, ever so slowly, but they are climbing. I am thankful for God's continuing grace as He teaches me more about patience than I ever wanted to learn. There are standing orders here to release me as soon as my numbers hit a certain level. This could be as early as tomorrow, so please join me in praying for that timing!

I am focused on an idea which is common at times like this: the desire for things to return to normal. There must have been something about normal that God wanted to change, or I would not be in this little room. I pray that God will give me the grace to change "normal" and the eyes to see exactly what He wants "normal" to look like now, for me.

Thank you again for your steadfast prayers; I know you are learning to "wait" along with me and I pray God will grow you as He has grown me.

Steve

Normal was good. Normal was pain-free. Normal was comfortable. Maybe it was too comfortable… so comfortable that it could stop me from stretching, reaching and moving forward in my relationship with a God who loves me enough to allow my faith to be tested.

When James writes to believers suffering "trials of various kinds" and speaks of letting the trial "have its full effect" (James 1:4 ESV), I do not think he expected them to go back to business as usual once the challenge had passed. James tells those believers, and us, that tests to our faith are intended to cause us to grow and change. When our faith is tested, we need to ask serious questions. What was the purpose of the trial? Why did God allow it into my life? How am I to grow from it? More importantly, we need to face the ordeal, not run from it. We can only grow by walking forward, into the midst of the storm, holding tightly to Jesus, even as our worlds split apart.

Believe me, I wanted to run. I do not like pain any more than the next guy. Many times, especially when the chemo was wrecking my body, I wanted to go back to "the good old days" before the trial, when everything was *normal.* But I trusted God that He was with me and that I needed to keep walking forward. That is what we need to focus on: trusting God in the midst of the storm; trusting Him to change our worlds for his purposes. When the storm ends, we need to ask God what our "new normal" should look like. I cannot tell you whether the changes will be drastic or subtle, but they will be important for you and your service to the King. James assures us that testing is intended to change us. He also tells us that God promises to give us wisdom if we seek it (James 1:5). We need to ask the questions honestly and be committed to embrace the changes in our lives that God intends.

This side of heaven, we may never understand all the "whys" for a particular time of testing. But we can act on the "whys" we do understand. Trials give us a laser-like focus, but such vision often fades over time. Use it while you have it. Step out in faith, ask God what needs to change, and then put those changes into place. Embrace them as your "new normal" from the hand of a loving Father who knows your heart better than you do yourself.

For me, the call is to put much less emphasis on certain things in my life that I thought were important and to redirect that time and energy into studying His Word, pursuing Him more passionately and passing on to others what He is showing me along the way. I never planned on writing a book about faith, but here I am writing. I never planned on speaking to groups about walking with God through cancer, but I have done that too. I have never felt so used by God to bring Him glory as I do now. I am hopefully beginning to grasp what Paul's "normal" looked like:

I have been crucified with Christ. It is no longer I who live, but Christ who lives in me. And the life I now live in the flesh I live by faith in the Son of God, who loved me and gave himself for me. (Galatians 2:20 ESV)

Been through your own personal storm recently? Embrace the *new* normal... what does it look like for you?

CHAPTER TWENTY

God's Timing

January 29

All: I know that you are all banging on the gates of heaven for me and I appreciate that so much. I am still here in the unit and likely will be here for a few more days, at the very least. This was not my plan, but it is clearly God's plan. We know that He is Lord over all. We also know that He is always faithful. But that does not mean that He is always faithful <u>on our timetable</u>. This is a hard thing for us to accept. Pray for me that I will be faithful in the waiting.

I love you all. Keep the prayers coming! I will be home soon, in His timing.

Steve

As I sat in the transplant unit waiting for my white cell counts to increase, one of the things I often heard from the doctors and nurses was, "another couple of days and you will be ready to go home." The first time I heard it, it was exciting. But to hear it day after day became maddening. I wanted God to act and I wanted Him to act now! I was past impatient, which is not difficult when we live in an instantaneous world with so much of what we want right at our fingertips.

Instantaneous is not God's typical pattern with His children. Ask Abraham, who searched for the Promised Land for decades, whether things were instantaneous. Ask Moses and the prophets whether they ever had to wait to hear God. Ask Peter and Paul whether God always worked on their timetables. He loved them just as He loves us; just as He loves you and me.

His love is certain; His timing is His own.

Peter describes our faith as gold being refined by the fires of testing (I Peter 1:6-7). Is a faith that demands instantaneous responses from God really faith at all? What good is a faith that cannot handle a delay? "Now faith is the assurance of things hoped for, the conviction of things not seen." (Hebrews 11:1 ESV) A faith that demands instant answers does not trust God's power or His character. You need a faith that can wait; a faith that trusts that He loves you, hears you and is able to answer your cry, even when the answers do not come. Your faith cannot be proven unless you experience delays and disappointments; waiting is part of the refining process intended to purify your faith.

Times of testing are meant to deepen our faith. Indeed, if He loves us, He will test us *if only to prove to us* that we have the ability to trust Him when facing our greatest fears. At the same time, as He answers our prayers, He also shows us that He is worthy of that faith, that it is well founded, and that He is who He says He is. His testing of our faith not only purifies us and our understanding of who God is, it ultimately gives Him glory in that He continues to reveal Himself to us as we come to trust Him more and more.

Waiting on God is not easy, but it is part of the process He uses to refine the believer: a process shown over and over again in Scripture. Be ready for the challenges that come your way and wait upon God's answers with a faith that is expectant, yet patient: a faith that is ready to grow.

CHAPTER TWENTY-ONE

Live Life at the Speed of God

February 1

All: God is gracious! He is letting me go home today! Rejoice with me and turn your prayers into praises for how He has been faithful to me and how He has taught me during my three-week stay. Thank you again, from the bottom of my heart, for all of your prayers for me.

My numbers are just barely at the level where my doctor feels that I can be safe in a controlled home environment, so I still need to be extremely careful. I cannot have visitors yet, so we will stay connected through email and the cell phone as we have for the last three weeks. But I am so thankful to be able to enjoy being at home! Please pray that the stem cells continue to en-graft into my bone marrow and produce tons and tons of white cells, red cells and platelets as they are designed to do. I want to get my numbers up as quickly as possible and get out of the dan-ger zone. Also, please increase your prayers for Becky, who now takes on the caregiver role! Yes, I will try to be a good patient!

A dear friend who recently went through her own stem cell transplant sent the following excerpt to me from a popular devotional book. Imagine God is speaking to you:

"Through the intimacy of our relationship, you are being transformed from the inside out. As you keep your focus on Me, I form you into the one I desire you to be. Your part is to yield to my creative work in you, neither resisting it nor trying to speed it up. Enjoy the tempo of a God-breathed life by letting Me set the pace. Hold My hand in childlike trust, and the way before you will open up step by step." (Hebrews 13:15, 2 Corinthians 3:18, Psalm 73:23-24.)

Sarah Young, Jesus Calling

The tempo of a God-breathed life, where we neither resist nor push… there is wisdom here my friends. Chew on it slowly. God has taught me so much while I have been here "on hold" for three weeks. Let Him change your heart and your life as He is changing mine. Do not resist His work in you!

Steve

This idea of pace and tempo in life was hitting me again. Let me take you back 30 days. I never could understand why God in His providence had delayed my entry into the transplant center for an entire week at the beginning of January. Didn't He know that my planned timing was perfect because of my lighter work schedule right after the first of the year? I was really upset! I wanted to get started and get it all over with before the pace of work picked up. I was losing time! I wouldn't get out until February! What was God doing?!?

Ever feel that way about changes in your schedule? The next time it happens, keep your eyes open and look for God's hand. We may have our plans, but He directs our steps (Proverbs 16:9).

In my case, that one-week delay enabled me, first of all, to be in the office and help resolve a situation where my personal input was critical. Then a second thing happened.

An attorney in town who was looking to change firms was referred to me by a common acquaintance. Our fields of specialization were similar, so if she were to move to our firm, she and I would be working closely together. She needed to know my situation, and I did not have much time before I would be out of commission for almost a month.

We were able to meet for lunch the day before I entered the transplant unit. In a short time, I shared the story of my cancer along with the story of my faith. She asked to be added to my email update list and told me that she would support me in prayer.

As she read my emails from the transplant unit, this woman saw me go through perhaps the hardest ordeal I had ever faced. She heard me tell of my struggles and the triumphs of faith from a unique perspective, since she had not known me before this time. She saw the same level of honest vulnerability that I was sharing with some of my closest friends and supporters who had known me for decades.

A couple of weeks after I was discharged, I asked her what she was thinking about her job move. Her words to me were, "I do not know a lot about your firm, but I certainly want to work with someone like you!" After meeting several of the other attorneys and staff at the firm, she discerned that many approached life with a similar perspective to mine. Within a couple of months, she chose us over other opportunities she had and moved her practice in with us.

I do not share this so that you think I must be a good guy to work with. I share this to show you what God can do with a frustrating delay in your planned schedule. Had she not been able to walk alongside me through my emails, she would not have gotten to know me on the inside in such a short period of time. God laid the groundwork for her decision through those emails: emails that she never would have seen had we not connected before I went into the transplant unit.

So, the next time your carefully planned schedule gets laid aside, keep your eyes open for what God may be doing in your life and in the lives of others. You may get the privilege of seeing His handiwork as it unfolds. He holds the keys to time itself in His hands. He has a plan for you and He moves in the lives of those around you (Jeremiah 29:11). If you are too focused on working *your* plan, you risk not seeing His.

I often pray that I will not run ahead of God, nor lag behind; I want to walk right beside Him.

Live life at the speed of God.

CHAPTER TWENTY-TWO

Perspective

February 6

All: It is hard to even explain how I felt coming home. Just the simple pleasure of riding in a car and seeing old familiar sites after three weeks in an isolation unit was almost overwhelming. I felt like a prisoner set free. Parts were surreal. Walking into my own house, sitting on my back porch, even just looking out the window into my neighborhood: all of it was wonderful and surreal at the same time. Praise God for such blessings that we too often take for granted. My capacity to appreciate the simple things has grown.

Since my release, I spend each morning sitting in a chair at my doctor's office hooked up to fluid lines and getting any other medications called for by the daily blood work. He had some concern that he was letting me out too early last Wednesday. My prayer that night was that the white cell counts would increase to a such level that on Thursday he would feel comfortable with his decision. And what happened? Our amazing God more than doubled them overnight!! It was incredible. And they have more than doubled again over the last few days!

Hopefully, all of my counts will continue to rise quickly so that the daily appointments can be cut back and I can have some normalcy in my schedule (as well as my wife's!).

As your week begins, know how much I appreciate your faithful prayers and encouragement. I will leave you with a little levity to start your week off with a smile: A mother was preparing pancakes for her sons, ages five and three. The boys began to argue over who would get the first pancake. Their mother saw the opportunity for a moral lesson so she said, "Now boys, if Jesus were sitting here, He would say, 'Let my brother have the first pancake. I can wait.'" The older brother turned to his younger brother and said, "You be Jesus."

We need to be like Jesus. Life is not about getting the first pancake!

Steve

When you go through a significant trial, you adopt one of two perspectives: your trial is either a random and unfortunate battle that you face with grim determination, or it is another chapter in your God-ordained journey. You have to fight either way, but as a Christian you can have confidence that He walks beside you. When I was having my transplant, there were other patients there who also knew the Lord. You could see it in their eyes. There was a remarkable level of peace. No, they were not enjoying the experience, but you could sense that they knew they were not alone, that God was right there with them in the midst of the struggle. You could sense an otherwise unexplainable strength that came from their faith.

Then there were others. Some with faces resolute, set hard as steel, and some who looked more like the proverbial deer in the headlights, anxious about what was coming next. I did not necessarily know what was coming any more than they did, but I knew I was not facing it alone. They may have had family beside them physically, just as I did, but I and others had Someone else. Someone who controls the universe.

How is it with you when you face a significant challenge that tests your faith? Did you gut the last one out or did you know your Father had you in His hands? If you gutted it out, relying on your own strength, how did that work for you? How will it be next time? You have a choice, you know. You can take God at His word that He will never leave you or forsake you (Deuteronomy 31:6; Hebrews 13:5). You can tell Him your fears and experience a peace beyond understanding (Philippians 4:6-7). It may not make your next trial a walk in the park, but your head will stay above the water and you will walk forward knowing that the time of testing has a purpose. (See James 1.)

I have often heard it said that going through cancer is a battle. I am sure it feels that way for those without the Lord. But with the Lord, it is a journey. You do not have to walk through the trial alone. Remember that the Lord is with you! When your next significant ordeal comes along, rest in these promises: He will never leave you. He is with you. He is using the trial in your life to teach you and to bring you closer to Him.

But if you would rather fight the battle in your own strength, go right ahead. I have to admit that I have tried that before myself.

I just hope you have a really good sword.

CHAPTER TWENTY-THREE

Hope Deferred

February 9

All: I am enjoying being at home and things are still improv-
ing with my counts! Thanks again for your prayers for me. My
doctor is pleased with my progress and is setting me up to have
the line in my chest taken out, since he will not need it any
longer to administer platelets or medications. This then paves
the way for restoration of my driving privileges! My immune
system still has a long way to go to full recovery, but by His
grace I continue to head in the right direction.

Thanks for your prayers,

Steve

Back when I was still in the hospital, as I waited, endlessly it seemed,
for my release from the hospital, God enhanced my understanding of hope
and, more importantly, the dangers associated with hopelessness. You can
probably quote Proverbs 13:12 to me: "Hope deferred makes the heart
sick, but a longing fulfilled is a tree of life." (NIV) After three weeks in
the transplant unit, being released was clearly a "tree of life" for me. Every

aspect of my existence seemed to improve the moment I exited those doors. But I remember how dismal my outlook had been just a week earlier, when I was still reeling from physical impacts of intense chemotherapy or the psychological impacts of isolation. Every day I waited for my blood counts to improve to the point where the doctors would allow me to go home, but it was slow. Had you asked me then whether I would do another transplant if I ever needed it again, I would have answered "no". No, even if it might again give me the best chance of an extended remission. My hope was beaten down. I fought against the thought that something might have gone wrong and my counts were never going to recover: that maybe I would never get out of the unit and back home.

Sound familiar? Have you ever been there, at that place of hopelessness? I know many of you have; some of you may be there even now.

We read in Psalm 121:1-2: "I will lift up my eyes to the mountains; from where shall my help come? My help comes from the LORD, who made heaven and earth." (ESV) There is only one source of hope. In those darkest moments, I simply grabbed hold of Jesus and held on. There was nothing else to hold onto and no one else who could understand where I was. Jesus could understand: He had been there, sweating great drops of blood, because the stress was so intense (Luke 22:44). This same Jesus promised never to leave me or forsake me (Hebrews 13:5). I simply had to trust Him in that promise.

He met me there in those dark moments, sometimes with an overwhelming comfort, sometimes strengthening me through His Word. The day that I felt sure my release would be approved, I was really depressed when I was told my numbers had simply not risen enough. The news was devastating. As I sat in my room, God sent a young man to see me, completely uninvited. Anthony was a music minister who visited the transplant unit to make the patients feel better. I had never even seen him before. He had visited several patients that day and was on his way out, but asked the charge nurse if there was anyone else he might see. She suggested he knock on my door. For the next twenty minutes, Anthony sang words of encouragement to me using contemporary Christian praise songs. Later that day, God sent a new nurse tech to my room, again a man I had never met before. Bernadin shared God's Word with me, just in casual conversation; words I needed to hear.

Regardless of what you are facing, He is faithful. He will not drop you. He will not stop listening to your cries. Just hold on. Keep your eyes open. Help will come.

CHAPTER TWENTY-FOUR

Refining Us Through Trial

February 18

All: It has been over two weeks since my release from the transplant unit. My counts continue to improve and the line that was inserted into an artery going directly into my heart has now been removed. My transplant doctor feels great about where I am and is transferring me back to my regular oncologist. This is all wonderful and shows that God is allowing me to make good progress. The only post-release problems that I've encountered have been two pesky rashes, neither of which bothered my transplant doctor, but both of which bothered me! He told me that this sometimes happens as the body recovers. It's like your body is simply blowing off steam and screaming, "What in the heck was all that about?!?" When I think of what I have put my body through in the last month or so, I can understand its frustration with me! The first rash was from waist to neck and passed within three days. The second is from my neck to the top of my now hairless head and seems to want to stay around and yell at me a little; pray that it might disappear like the first one did!

I still cannot be around a lot of people, but I have gotten my driving privileges back. This is a blessing in that it takes a load off Becky, who now no longer has to cart me around to my appointments. I am very blessed to have had a chauffeur and caretaker who never complained even if the appointment was really early in the morning!

I will leave you with a verse quoted by Charles Spurgeon in his morning devotional for today. This powerful verse is from a poem by William Cowper:

> *Trials make the promise sweet,*
> *Trials give new life to prayer.*
> *Trials bring me to His feet,*
> *Lay me low, and keep me there.*

Stay at His feet, my brothers and sisters, and grow.

Steve

Sometimes growth seems immediate, like those times when we say afterwards, "Wow, I'll never do that again!" At other times God is changing us in ways that are harder to see. We are growing either way. We can feel a little lost in the process, when God is working to change us over a long period of time. Feeling lost is okay; you will see the change eventually. Others may see it even before you do. The gold is in the furnace and the dross is being removed.

Paul tells us that he prayed for the church in Philippi, "being confident in this, that he who began a good work in you will carry it on to completion." (Philippians 1:6 NIV) God reaches down to us while we are lost in our sin and begins a work in our hardened hearts that will ultimately enable us to reflect the heart of Jesus. This is the process of sanctification: the life-long, God-orchestrated changes that transform us from sinners to saints. Paul understood this process. He knew God's boundless grace and love for us and that He would stick with the task until it was completed to His satisfaction. This is how Paul could pray confidently that the love among the Philippian believers would abound, that they would grow in discernment of the truth and the fruits of righteousness, and that it would all be for the glory of God (1:9-11).

How are you handling the changes that God is bringing to pass in your life? Do you look forward to them with anticipation or are you fighting them at every turn? Very few of us enjoy change, especially if we are comfortable where we are at the moment. But none of us are where we need to be, no matter how much we have grown along the paths where God has led us. I am always amazed to hear Paul cry out, "Wretched man that I am! Who will deliver me from this body of death?" (Romans 7:24 ESV)

Why my amazement? This is Paul! If there is anyone I hold up as an example of fighting the fight, enduring the afflictions, understanding the gospel and reflecting the love of Christ to his enemies in the face of severe persecution, it is the apostle Paul. How can he see himself as wretched?

Paul knew the truth. He knew that the more we grow in our walk and our relationship with the Holy Father, the more we will see what still needs to change: the more we will see the dross, the impurities and the wretchedness. Paul knew well the recurring Old Testament image of the refiner's fire, of gold and silver being purified in the furnace.

But who can endure the day of his coming? Who can stand when he appears? For he will be like a refiner's fire or a launderer's soap. He will sit as a refiner and purifier of silver; he will purify the Levites and refine them like gold and silver. Then the Lord will have men who will bring offerings in righteousness and the offerings of Judah and Jerusalem will be acceptable to the Lord, as in days gone by, as in former years. (Malachi 3:2-4 NIV)

References to purification by fire or being refined occur also in Proverbs 25:4; Isaiah 1:25; Jeremiah 9:7; Daniel 11:35, 12:10. Paul repeats this image in I Corinthians 3:13-15 and reminds us that the quality of our own works will be tested by fire. We are being refined so that our offerings can be presented from purified hearts, in righteousness, for God's glory.

Trials are our furnace. (See I Peter 1:6-7.) All praise to a God who starts a good work in us out of His pure grace and does not give up on us.

Embrace the trial. Embrace the change. Sanctification is occurring, whether you see it yet or not.

If He loves you, and He does, He will change you. He will finish the work He began in your heart.

CHAPTER TWENTY-FIVE

Change Takes Time

March 1

All: I was "nudged" yesterday to get another update out, so here it is. There is not a great deal to update you on. I am still working from home and avoiding the office and any crowded situations. I have had a few one-on-one or small group meetings at lunch in open-air venues. This has been great to get me reconnected to clients and folks in the office and a welcome break from relative isolation. The skin rash still lingers, but one of my doctors has now suggested that I drop one of my medications on the theory that my new immune system may be reacting to it differently than my old system did. I have been on this medication since last August and did not suspect it as the culprit. But, with a rebooted immune system, things can change. Ah, the journey continues still!

The phrase "things can change" could be the title of a book that any of us could write. I think back to where I was last spring and, more particularly, where my heart and my head were. God allowed changes in my body to cause other, more important, changes. He needed to get my attention, and cancer

*is what He allowed in order to spur His desired changes in my
heart and head. I do not believe that He desired to bring pain
into my life, but He is certainly using it to accomplish His purposes. We are told that "in all things God works for the good of
those who love Him" (Rom 8:28 NIV), and I believe that verse
now more than ever before.*

*Thanks again for your continued prayers and I hope to see
many of you soon!*

Steve

A cancer diagnosis will stop you in your tracks. It will immediately
change your life, as all of your plans and dreams are put on hold.

Sometimes God needs to put our plans on hold. Consider Paul's experience on the Damascus road in Acts 9. Do you think God got his attention? Do you think Paul's plans changed? How about when Moses had to
flee Egypt (Exodus 2:15)? Do you think it changed his life plan? The Bible
is full of similar examples. Look at the stories of Joseph being betrayed by
his brothers or Mary's life after she encountered the Angel Gabriel.

We all have a tendency to put these characters from Scripture up on
pedestals. Much respect is due them. But we need to keep firmly in mind
that they were men and women just like us. They had hopes and dreams
and plans just as you and I do. Those plans, however, were all changed in
a moment, because God had a bigger plan, a grander plan… a plan that
they would not have believed had He told them Himself. (See Habakkuk
1:5.) It was part of God's plan to use them for His eternal purposes. He
has purposes for you and me as well. I'm not making myself — or you
— their equal, but we need to be equally willing to be used. My point is
that God works in all of our lives to cause changes in our hearts for His
purposes. If you truly want to be used by Him and for His purposes, He
will change you.

Any significant change takes time. God took Paul into Arabia for three
years to prepare him for his ministry to the Gentiles. God allowed Joseph

to experience years of hardship, including servitude and prison, to change him into the man who would ultimately save all of Egypt and the Israelites during a worldwide famine. Moses fled the house of Pharaoh to spend years as a desert shepherd, as God changed his heart to return to Egypt as the deliverer of the Israelites. Change simply takes time.

It troubles us that we cannot clearly see all points on the path ahead and where change is taking us. But Scripture suggests that we are, perhaps, to look only for the next step, not the whole path. (See Psalm 119:105; Proverbs 16:9.) I am learning more of patience; change and growth take time. The productive side of me is frustrated that I do not feel like I am "doing" much during this season, but I need to leave that in His hands. Since this journey started, one of my continuing prayers is that He would enable me to do those good works which He prepared beforehand for us to do (Ephesians 2:10). If He is going to answer that prayer, there may be many things that need changing or building inside of me. I need to trust that He is working, whether I can see it clearly or not. Time will show me the results of His work. My job is to be patient, available, and open to His changes in me for His greater purposes.

What about you? What winds of change do you feel blowing into your life? Be open to His changes… they are for your good… and, ultimately, for His glory.

CHAPTER TWENTY-SIX

When Trials Subside

March 19

Good morning my brothers and sisters! I hope that this week is starting off well for you. My last blood tests (over a week ago) showed good improvement in the numbers. I go in for another test this Friday and would covet your prayers that the good reports continue and that my counts are all even stronger. This Friday I will also need to make some decisions about what type of maintenance chemotherapy to use going forward, to keep the cancer in remission. Although the dosages will be smaller than last fall, I must admit some anxiety about returning to any form of chemo. I have enjoyed the past months of not pouring poison into my system! Please pray that God will give wisdom to me and to my oncologist concerning which drug to use, since there are several choices.

As you may expect from the fact that my updates are getting farther and farther apart, some "normalcy" is creeping back into my life. I am reconnecting with friends and clients, my energy is returning, and I am beginning to work longer hours each week. Things are "getting back to normal." Sounds great, doesn't it? So why am I beginning to feel a little more distant from Christ? Why am I finding that it takes a lot more discipline to be in prayer; not just rote prayer and going through some list of requests, but real heartfelt, fervent prayer? I find my mind straying to those same distractions that competed for my affections before cancer: distractions that quickly showed themselves to be valueless in the face of a new and stark reality.

Let me encourage you today, even at this moment, to take the extra time to be alone with Him. Drive deeper into prayer and avoid just going through the motions. Don't let daily distractions rob you of what is most important.

And the next time you see me, please remind me to do the same.

Steve

Any significant affliction will test our faith. But when the trial ends and the pressure is off, a different challenge appears: a more subtle — yet no less dangerous — challenge to our walk with God.

In the midst of being barraged with pain, loss, fear, or despair, we cling to Christ and His promises. We spend extra time in prayer and in His Word, looking for answers or longing for strength. Why does it take a desert experience to bring us to this level of spiritual activity? Why are we not always spending extended time in prayer, looking for those extra few minutes where we can read the Bible, seeking a deeper relationship with a loving God?

As I write this, my walk with cancer has taken me through chemo, radiation and a stem cell transplant. I have felt frustration, depression, and the anxiety of not knowing whether cancer will appear again. Yet words cannot express the intimate presence of God that I have felt during this Psalm 23 "walk through the valley." Since I am in remission now, with a well-founded hope that I can stay in remission for a long time, things are "getting back to normal." Isn't that great?

Maybe. Then again, maybe not.

Look at Deuteronomy 8. Moses recounts how God led the Israelites through the desert for 40 years, how he humbled them, taught them to obey and protected them during the process. He describes the Promised Land that they are about to enter and how God has lovingly provided for them streams of water, fruit trees, and lush fields for their livestock: a land where they will lack nothing. But then he warns them: after you leave the desert and begin to enjoy all of the fruits of the Promised Land, do not forget that it all comes from God's hand; do not forget to continue to honor and obey Him as you did in the desert.

Here is the point: Things can go downhill if we forget. Do not forget God when the trials are absent and when everything is going well.

Things in my world are beginning to ease up... and it scares me a little. Does the ease in your life scare you? It should. You may be in a dangerous place where you can easily forget your complete dependence on God. And you may not even realize it.

Pursue God with every moment you have and do not waste time on distractions. Paul tells us in II Timothy 2:4 that a good soldier does not waste time on civilian pursuits, spending his efforts on things that will not make a difference in his service to his commander. He knows the battles are coming. So do you. Sharpen your sword while you have time. Get your armor ready. Your next battle could start tomorrow.

CHAPTER TWENTY-SEVEN

Getting Back to Normal

April 4

Good morning! I appreciate all of the prayers concerning my decision a couple of weeks ago about the maintenance medication. I have decided to go the pill-a-day route as opposed to weekly injections or an even less frequent, but higher dose, alternative. I will start the pills later this week. This will be a new chemotherapy drug that I have not had before, so I would appreciate prayers that I would have no side effects. The initial regimen is one pill a day for 21 days, then 7 days off. It is daunting to consider that this regimen could continue for the rest of my life, barring new advances in medications. But, as they say, it beats the alternative! I have certainly learned that every day is precious and that a little pill thrown in is inconsequential, especially if it helps to keep the cancer in remission. I will actually be taking a total of 4 pills a day, counting the two protective drugs I have been on since this started last summer, and an additional pill meant to counteract a potential side effect of the new maintenance drug. Ah, the wonders of medicine… better living through chemistry!

I am experiencing more normalcy every week, spending more time in the office and connecting with folks that I have not seen or spoken to in months. This is all wonderful. I am still fighting the balance battle that I mentioned last time; as normalcy creeps in, it is harder to hang on to the intimacy I experienced with God in the transplant center. Distractions are keeping me from focusing on listening to God.

April 19

My dear friends: Another two weeks have passed and I am pleased to report that I am not experiencing any additional side effects from the new medication! Praise God for that blessing! I am continuing to have some ongoing skin issues that are either a holdover from the transplant or somehow related to something I am taking. Nothing has gotten worse, but some aspects that I thought would improve have not. It is manageable, even if a little frustrating. I am still learning patience through this aspect of the journey and that is yet another reason to be thankful.

In response to my last couple of emails, some of you have responded to me with great wisdom on <u>appreciating</u> normalcy. One good friend wrote:

*"God is **all for** normal; it's what He promises His people. The wife of your youth, and the children of your loins; the oil of joy, and the new wine of gladness: "Every man will sit under his own vine and under his own fig tree." (Micah 4:4 NIV) True, these things are only the shadow of greater peace to come — but when you've <u>got</u> blessings, you can be sure they come from God. And your other priorities come from God, too."*

Thanks again for your continuing prayers. Thanks also to those of you who are pouring into me in special ways along this continuing adventure.

Steve

So what do you do at the end of a trial — or at the end of a mountain-top experience? Both are settings where we hear God as never before, and both get our attention. But what do you do when it is over? Do you just go back to your daily routine? What do you do with what just happened?

When Moses came down from Mount Sinai with the two tablets of the Testimony in his hands, he was not aware that his face was radiant because he had spoken with the LORD. (Exodus 34:29 NIV)

Then Jesus was led by the Spirit into the desert to be tempted by the devil... Then the devil left him, and angels came and attended him... When Jesus heard that John had been put in prison, he returned to Galilee. (Matthew 4:1, 11-12 NIV)

There he was transfigured before them. His face shone like the sun, and his clothes became as white as the light. (Matthew 17:2 NIV)

As I began to recover following the transplant, I started working again. It was slow at first, but as my strength returned I worked more and more each week. What I began to notice was that the intimacy I had felt with God in the transplant unit began to fade, and this troubled me greatly. I lamented to the friend mentioned above that I did not want to go back to normal and lose that intimacy. We went back and forth in several emails. I talked about going out into the desert, or up onto the mountaintop as Moses did, and finding an intimacy that I longed for after the experience was over. He reminded me of a great truth:

But we don't **stay** in the desert, any more than Jesus did. I'm convinced that God doesn't intend for us to do so. We go out into the desert for a period – whether voluntarily or because God leads us there; then we take what we've learned there and let it shape how we live *"in the land your God is giving you."* That land, the place of blessing, is where we live; notice how the Bible always says we go <u>out</u> from there to the wilderness... and then come back.

We are not to return from the desert unchanged. Moses' face may have faded, but I bet he was never the same after his experience on the mountain. His faith was stronger, his assurance greater. The next time he was tempted to doubt, it was almost certainly easier to believe and to obey in full confidence. His idea of God was bigger, and his capacity to be used by God was bigger as well. He remembered his experience, with profit. You and I will, too. But we can't waste our time trying to recreate the experience; the point is to use it.

Did you get that? **He remembered his experience, with profit; he used it.** This is a great lesson we all need to remember. When God takes the time to pour into your life in a special way, do not waste the opportunity. Let it change you and use it for His glory. Let it become part of your story, part of your testimony. Remember, it is ultimately not about us, but about Him. He does not pour wisdom and experience into us for our glorification, but for His own.

The desert and mountaintop experiences will come and go; we do not remain there. Part of the reality of not staying there is that the emotional side of the experience may fade. But the things we learn there — the wisdom He imparts, the faith that He builds, the changes in our hearts — these do not need to fade. We need to remember them, use them, weave them into our souls and pass them along to others. God gives us incredible opportunities to share our experiences right where He has placed us in our "normal" daily lives. These are opportunities to glorify Him and bless others with our testimony of what an awesome God can do and has done in our lives.

I have a dear friend who has just started his own cancer journey. I have been walking alongside him. I would have done that even if I did not have cancer. But now I can do it differently, because I know the journey myself. What God has done in my life can help my brother. God has given me a new platform for ministry among those who hurt and those who fear. I know that feeling of hopelessness and I have learned that you can trust God in that place. My heart has been changed.

He has not touched your life for you alone. Reach out to those who are walking the path that you have walked. Share their pain. Tell them what God has shown you; breathe new life into their hurting world.

Remember our Savior who entered into *our* pain to bring *us* life. In your own way, do the same for someone else who is hurting.

CHAPTER TWENTY-EIGHT

What I Have Learned

May 18

All: I had follow-up appointments over the last week and a half with both my oncologist and my transplant doctor. Both were pleased with my blood tests and overall recovery from the transplant. I am now on a six-week follow-up cycle with the oncologist, and the transplant doctor does not want to see me until my one-year anniversary in January. They both told me to feel free to get back into the mainstream and do anything I want. As I continue with the maintenance chemotherapy, I will obviously still need to be careful, but it is good to have the full green light. This is great news and continuing evidence of God's blessing and mercy.

I was privileged last evening to deliver the opening prayer at the 2012 Lifework Leadership Graduation ceremony in Orlando. Before I prayed, I shared a little of my own story, especially what I had experienced during the last year. I hope that it encouraged them to allow God to change them through their own challenges, as He has changed me through mine.

This is a continuing journey, and I could not have made it this far without your prayers. I can never say thank you enough. Many of you have encouraged me to find a way to somehow put my emails into print to be shared with others. I want you to know that I am working on that; please continue your prayers that God would lead me as to how to put it together. Others of you have encouraged me to continue to write down what God continues to say to me as my journey continues. I am working on that as well. A good friend recently felt led by the Holy Spirit to kick me off the fence, so he simply set up a blog site for me and said, "get going!" Shortly, I will send out another email and give you the site address and invite you to come along, if you wish.

As both of our journeys continue, please know how much I appreciate having each one of you alongside me on mine.

Steve

Many of you may be unfamiliar with the group Lifework Leadership, whom I was so proud to address. For the past twenty years, the group (formerly Greater Orlando Leadership Foundation) has provided a nine-month leadership training program aimed at emerging Christian leaders in the marketplace. Orlando now has over 800 graduates and sister programs have started in several other major cities in the US. It is an amazing work of God. Here is what I said to them as I shared a bit of my journey with God through cancer:

"When you walk along this path you learn deeper lessons. You learn in a deeper way that God is real and that He reigns over all of life. You learn in a deeper way that He hears you when you call out to Him. You see Him answer your prayers in ways that are so immediate and so personal that He becomes virtually tangible.

"In March, I started on a maintenance program of low dose chemo-therapy coupled with a few other medications, all of which, by God's grace,

I am tolerating well. This maintenance program will likely continue for the next several years. My cancer is not a type that you remove; it is a type that you try to control. My journey is a continuing one; so is yours.

"James tells us that when we go through a trial, we need to let the trial have its full effect, that we may become perfect and complete, lacking in nothing. This journey is changing the way I think, the way I understand and relate to God, the way I look at life and my calling in His service.

"God has had those of you in this graduating class on a journey for the last nine months. My prayer for you is that you will let it have its full effect! Build on what you have learned and experienced. Let it change you. Do not go back to the way you thought nine months ago, the way you prioritized your life nine months ago, or the way you understood and related to God nine months ago. Use all that you have learned and experienced to propel you forward to serve the Risen King wherever He has placed you and wherever He may take you in life... as your journey continues."

My prayer for you, dear reader, is the same: allow every experience that God brings into your life to change you into who He wants you to be... who He created you to be.

Epilogue

So, now you know why I wrote this book: to share the story of God's faithfulness to me through the storm of an unexpected disease. My belief and confidence in the God of the Old and New Testaments is light years past where it was in the summer of 2011. My experience has not changed my theology; it has made it real. I had walked with God for years, but on pretty level paths. He took me on a new journey. It was not one I wanted, but to experience His deep, faithful presence is a priceless treasure. I would make the trade again tomorrow, even though I shudder at the thought.

I tell people that I am stronger than I was in the summer of 2011, but still not as strong as I thought I was; that was pride. Where am I now? Hopefully, at a place with less pride and more humility: deeper understanding and more trust.

God will keep you safe and speak to you in the midst of your storms too, but you have to reach out to Him. Matthew 7:7-8 tells us that if we seek Him, we will find Him. He is real and He is near. Call to Him and he will answer you. He has spoken to me, revealed Himself, and touched me in ways that make it impossible to doubt His existence or His constant presence.

I have multiple myeloma. The doctors tell me that it always comes back. Throughout this journey, God's faithfulness to me and my family has been constant. As I said in previous chapters, James encourages us to count it a blessing when we experience a challenge that tests our faith and to let the experience transform us, making us better servants to the King. I walk forward trusting that His blessings and His work inside me will continue. If the cancer comes back, it will not change who He is; it will just be another part in the journey.

I hope that this book has somehow helped you. If it did, pass it on or tell others about it. If you are interested in hearing more of what God continues to teach me as my journey continues, please visit my blog: <u>www.stephenbhatcher.com</u> and sign up to follow my story. I would love to hear your comments on the book or any of my blog posts.

Be blessed and trust the God who hears us.

Steve

About the Author

Steve Hatcher is a man who has experienced God's grace. He is a cancer survivor who is simply navigating a road that he did not expect to ever walk down. Steve is happily married to an incredible woman who walks beside him, wonderfully proud of his two sons, thankful for two amazing daughters-in-law and enraptured with his granddaughter. Steve keeps an eye on her little finger, making sure that he does not get wrapped around it, which would not be good for him or for her.

Steve holds degrees from Rhodes College, Vanderbilt University School of Law and the University of Florida Graduate Tax Program. He has practiced law in Orlando, Florida for over thirty years.